Praise for *The Power of Naming*

"It is said in the Native American world that 'wisdom sits in places.' Just a few pages into this glorious and empowering book, I could see the truth in that for myself. Wisdom sits in this place, inside these pages. Rarely have I felt so supported in reading a book. The author guides and challenges us with a masterful hand, a loving heart, and a knowing beyond knowing that this journey toward our own naming is both life affirming and treacherous. This is the book and the guide I've been waiting for."
— Patti Digh, author of *Life Is a Verb*

"Writing from her ferocious passion for stepping into the fullness of who we are and reclaiming our innate power and wisdom, Melanie DewBerry takes us on a journey deep inside to uncover our true, vibrant, wise, and creative selves."
— Alan Seale, author of *Soul Mission, Life Vision* and *Create a World That Works*

THE
PWER
OF
NAMING

Hay House Titles of Related Interest

YOU CAN HEAL YOUR LIFE, the movie,
starring Louise Hay & Friends
(available as a 1-DVD program and an expanded 2-DVD set)
Watch the trailer at: www.LouiseHayMovie.com

THE SHIFT, the movie,
starring Dr. Wayne W. Dyer
(available as a 1-DVD program and an expanded 2-DVD set)
Watch the trailer at: www.DyerMovie.com

ARCHETYPES: Who Are You?, by Caroline Myss

*COURAGEOUS DREAMING: How Shamans Dream the World
into Being,* by Alberto Villoldo, Ph.D.

*MEET YOUR SOUL: A Powerful Guide to Connect with Your
Most Sacred Self,* by Elisa Romeo

THE 7 SECRETS OF SOUND HEALING, by Jonathan Goldman

*YOUR 3 BEST SUPER POWERS: Meditation, Imagination &
Intuition,* by Sonia Choquette

All of the above are available at your local
bookstore, or may be ordered by visiting:

Hay House USA: www.hayhouse.com®
Hay House Australia: www.hayhouse.com.au
Hay House UK: www.hayhouse.co.uk
Hay House South Africa: www.hayhouse.co.za
Hay House India: www.hayhouse.co.in

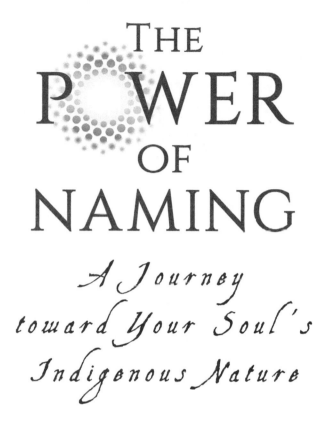

THE
P WER
OF
NAMING

A Journey toward Your Soul's Indigenous Nature

MELANIE DEWBERRY

HAY HOUSE, INC.
Carlsbad, California • New York City
London • Sydney • Johannesburg
Vancouver • New Delhi

Published and distributed in the United States by: Hay House, Inc.: www.hayhouse.com® • *Published and distributed in Australia by:* Hay House Australia Pty. Ltd.: www.hayhouse.com.au • *Published and distributed in the United Kingdom by:* Hay House UK, Ltd.: www.hayhouse. co.uk • *Published and distributed in the Republic of South Africa by:* Hay House SA (Pty), Ltd.: www.hayhouse.co.za • *Distributed in Canada by:* Raincoast Books: www.raincoast.com • *Published in India by:* Hay House Publishers India: www.hayhouse.co.in

Cover design: Amy Rose Grigoriou
Interior design: Pamela Homan

Cataloging-in-Publication Data is on file with the Library of Congress

Tradepaper ISBN: 978-1-4019-5001-9

10 9 8 7 6 5 4 3 2 1
1st edition, April 2017

Printed in the United States of America

SUSTAINABLE FORESTRY INITIATIVE

Certified Sourcing
www.sfiprogram.org
SFI-01268

SFI label applies to text stock only

CONTENTS

INTRODUCTION

This book is not intended for the faint of heart. It is for women and men who are ready to remember who they are, for those who are done with trying to be everything to everyone, done with living from past events, and done with not being exactly who they are. Women are constantly told that their value lies in their beauty or how much they can give to another. Men are told to downplay their spirituality and that emotions are a no-no. Though you know this isn't true, it's easy to get lost in the story of nature. You were never meant to conform or to fit your vast wild nature into a slip of an existence.

Working through these chapters, you will encounter the ways in which you were asked to hide from your soul's identity. Then, you will fiercely reclaim it. You will burn to the ground those imposed versions of you that kept you from your certain knowing. You will take a stand for your authority. You will uncover your name and live as the divine blessing that you have always been.

The work that is required is demanding and it is confronting, but it is also freeing. This is the path of the spiritually brave. This is not the path of a warrior, where one has to fight to move forward. This is the walk home to yourself.

Do your best. You will know if you've put your heart and soul into it, or if you've taken shortcuts. You will have to let go of how you learn to receive this work. But don't worry: You are up for the challenge. You will find you have more creative imagination than you have known. This is the gift that freedom brings. This work will challenge your fear and champion your soul.

The Practices

Each chapter takes you through a process of rediscovery. And at the end of each chapter, there is a practice. These practices are not for the linear mind; they are for your *soul*. Take your time, but don't procrastinate. Yes, there is work to be done, so do the work. You don't need to process it, intellectualize it, or even understand it. You just need to *want* yourself to be whole.

They are called "practices" (as opposed to "exercises") because we are always in the practice of becoming. These are not mere exercises; they are ways to create an enfolding of you in all you are and all you will become. This is the practice of walking as the Named One. The Named One is the one who lives from divine alignment. The one who no longer negotiates or compromises any aspect of themselves to fit in or be liked. The Named One lives from love, self-love, and the love of other, and love never negotiates. Each day, we begin anew in the practice of living as the Named One. When you arrive at the practice, you may need to check to see that it is really YOU who is doing it. You may find it helpful to spend five minutes breathing, slowly creating a meditative state before you begin. I encourage you to do each practice in one sitting. It is worth repeating to be wary of the thought that you should put the work down and come back to it later. This is the negative mind attempting to delay you from your knowing.

I encourage you to get a journal to record your insights. It will be helpful to review all you've stripped away and all you have found inside when it comes time to be named.

Journey Well

This is the *journey to your soul's identity*. How far you go and what you experience is up to you. You can decide now to be wholly who you are. You can decide now to surrender yourself to the real truth your soul and mind have for you and to allow their truth complete dominion. You can decide now to no longer postpone your fulfillment. You can decide now to create a specific hour several times a week to meet yourself between these pages. You can decide now to block off time and practice saying no to intrusions to one of the most important pieces of work you've ever done. You can decide now to desire yourself fully, honoring your divine longing for the congruence awaiting. You can decide now that peace is your birthright. You can decide now to recognize how thirsty you've been for this reckoning and give yourself the water of life. Everything good starts with a conscious decision.

As you move through each chapter, you step closer to your name. You will be released from the need either to rebel against the labels given to you (a.k.a., being named by others) or to surrender in defeat and attempt to fit into those labels. You will experience that living as the Named One puts you at the helm of authenticity. Old behaviors that you've not been able to shake—the many ways in which you have negotiated your true identity so you will be liked and accepted, your lack of clearly defined boundaries, your need to control, or being told what to think or do so you have no control—will fall away. You were not birthed to spend your energy adjusting your soul's expansiveness to fit in a small, reductionist label. As you seek your name, all who you are—your dark, dangerous nature, your beauty, your brilliance—comes together to walk you back to your original home, to love and to your soul. Whatever your name is, be assured that you came into this world complete, with courage and the power to love and to be loved. You are a risk-taker who is primed for your destiny as an ever-evolving spirit. Whoever you are, whatever your name, you were born to live in congruence with your soul; doing so will bring all the peace you've ever wanted and all that the world has ever needed.

As you work through the chapters of this book, your name will call you forward without compromise or second-guessing. And when you and your name reunite, you will experience yourself freed, loved, and aligned with your highest self. Be honest with what you say and write. Say what you know is true without a disclaimer. Tell the truth. The truth will soothe you and bring you peace. No one thinks you're arrogant or being too much—no one relevant, that is. Take risks here. Do you want this new beginning? If you do, this work will challenge all that your ego holds dear. You will have to take risks. You will be walking up to the face of lies. This is not always easy; many do not take this walk. Many people want to "be done to." They want someone to fix them, as though that is possible, letting the astrologer, the coach, the therapist do it externally. What you desire can only be procured by you. How else will you know the depth of your soul, the level of your commitment, the vastness of your beauty if you don't experience it? You are no one's victim. Fill these pages by staying present to yourself. Don't go away mentally, physically, or spiritually as much as you may want to. Take a stand to stay. Stay. Stay like you've never stayed before. Should you feel tired and want to stop, know that is the first destination the ego will take you to. In your mind, it will sound like, *This is boring; I know this already; I'll come back to it later; I'm not sure this is relevant; I just want the name—I can skip this. This is too confrontational.* The ego is cunning enough to make you believe these are your own thoughts. Don't go back to sleep, stay. Stay awake and press on. The journey has begun.

Listen to your interior self, for it has been waiting to share your own wisdom with you. Listen well and record it. Write down what you hear and visit what you have captured often. Don't trust your mind to recall those profound pieces of wisdom. Your mind is up against a lifetime of lies and absence. Verbalize what you hear and what you dare. Saying it aloud will enable your eardrum to literally drum it into your psyche. Care compassionately for yourself. Change is challenging, so rest well. Eat well. Laugh often and only share the work you do with those who can hold your precious evolving nature with love and tenderness. This is one of the very first practices for you to learn. Never give someone who has only an espresso-size cup a latte cup's worth of your insight. Take care of your spirit. One way to do this is to go out in nature. Even in the winter, you can find a way to visit nature. You can always have a conference call with the Star Nation. (*Star Nation* is a Native American term we use to speak about the stars.)

When you live your name, you live the love and peace that have always been with you.

Ready or Knot

Here in the naming realm, your fight becomes complete. The honoring of you is about to begin. We, the world, are ready for who you are, or we are not. You may be ready for what is asked of you to unearth your name, or not. *Ready* is one of those words we use to mean "If my fear is about to dissolve or give me the go-ahead, then I will move forward." The idea of being ready keeps most people from taking the next step in their life. Fear becomes their knot. When an elder comes to us to tell us to participate in a ceremony, they do so because they see we are in need—otherwise known as ready. They never ask if we are ready. We accept their vision for us and begin preparing ourselves. Sit with your soul and listen. It is calling you forward. A willingness is what is required to be named. Be prepared for your will to navigate through your fear. You will be asked to lay down all forms of protection that you have used to hide yourself from you. You will delete ways in which your beautiful nature was interrupted. You cannot understand or intellectualize your way into being you. You cannot prepare life in such a fashion that you know what will come and how. You can only be willing to say yes to life. Show up ready to meet it again and again. The truth of who you are—your name—doesn't wait for you to be ready. Your desires are all the invitation you need. If you're reading this book, some part of you wants the whole of you to be ready and willing. My question to you is not, Are you ready? It's, Are you wanting? Do you desire emotional and spiritual agility? Isn't now the time to experience freedom from doubt and compliance? Take off your mask. You are safe. It is safe for you to live your life. These chapters hold a pathway not only to your archetypal name but to a way of walking in the world that is aligned with your name.

Take It All Off

Being named is a journey. On the Red Road (Native American spirituality), my elders say, "It's not always easy, but it is good." Your journey may not be easy at every turn, but it will always bring richer soil and a deeper rooting of you. At some level, we all know who we are, yet we became masterful at masquerading ourselves as requested by others. This was our survival plan at work. It's time now to come out of your bunkered self.

It's time to look at the ways you might have masked yourself. It's time to look at what treasures you have denied, hidden, or fought for us to see. You may find some of the clues in your dark side, the shadow. We don't go near the shadow enough. Just the word *shadow* begs to be avoided. We'll unlock the shadow closet further down the road.

What you name yourself to be, consciously or unconsciously, will create your life experiences. Not admitting who you are tells a story too, albeit an unconscious one. The power to admit who you are is yours, as is the power to deny. That is what it is to have choice. Refuse the call to your soul's identity and you will remain stuck. This is a state of absolute suffering. Suffering is not on the docket. If you have been stuck, this work will help you pry yourself free.

Yes, it takes courage to speak the truth. Courage doesn't come easy, but it will make you rich in spirit. Isn't that a beautiful way to be wealthy? To know you gave your heart and soul to it all and left nothing off the table? Courage takes practice. Again and again you will be asked to practice yourself into consciousness. Life is a series of practices that become your certain evolution. You will evolve. You will have access to more of your inner beauty, and this will make all the difference. If the snake refuses to shed her skin, she dies. There is no growth without the tear of old skins. The first step you will take is of shedding, to identify all the ways in which you've protected your truth. You don't need the false sense of protection of the past. Truth needs no protection. It needs your voice. Let your wisdom strip away anything that keeps you from your name. Admit you want freedom, and go be it.

You may decide to do this work with other like-minded souls. I highly recommend group work. Gather to support one another but do your own work and don't allow yourself to be overly influenced by the insights of others. Share what feels comfortable to share and hold off on the parts that you're not ready to share or receive feedback on. Group work can make the hard to do possible with love and creativity. Too often we are on the spiritual path alone. Circle up! Gather around the fire of the heart to be held. In my Native community, many of our ceremonies are done together because the work is taxing as we dig deep to touch the soul and evade the lure of the ego. Together we are there to support one another. We may not even speak to one another, but our physical and spiritual presence inspires us to stay in the practice of the ceremony. There is something beautiful about a group of beings walking a spiritual path together. You can see yourself more clearly as you witness others moving along their paths.

However you do this work, to hear and elicit your name you will need to be honest with yourself and admit that deep down inside you have always had at least an inkling of your essence, but you've played a game of hide-and-seek with your soul. You hide the truth of "you" and seek it when it is safe to be you in the world. You are not alone; everyone is playing the same game. Each chapter is designed to take you deeper within yourself. First, you begin by identifying the obstacles that keep you from hearing your beauty. After you have cleared some of those roadblocks, you will work to reclaim your organic nature, to admit and walk proudly in your beauty. You will be asked to become nonnegotiable with your spirit and to stand in love. Naming is a process of undoing first and seeking within later.

The Origins of Soul Naming: The Red Road

The work I've done with naming clients is born out of the journey I've taken along the Red Road. The Red Road is the Native American spiritual path. Though I am of Cherokee and Choctaw descent, my elders' teachings are drawn from the Lakota people. My chief, Joe Chasing His Horse, was asked to bring the Lakota sacred ceremonies to the Dinè (Navajo) reservation in Big Mountain, Arizona, to help the Dinè people maintain their strength as their lands were being stripped by the coal mining industry. It was on this mountain more than 25 years ago that I began my walk on this road. I am taught to honor the earth's wisdom, to be open to change as the earth does with each season, to humbly respect and care for all life with remembrance of their scared nature, and to honor my own sacredness. I participate in our traditional ceremonies that remake me, open my heart, and are a conduit to my soul's voice. The Red Road and the teachings of my elders Andrea and Pablo Lopez, have given me the strength to move in the direction of love in a world that seems to not always be loving.

We Belong to One Another

A common prayer you would hear on this road is Mita-kuye Oyasin ("We Are All Related" or "All My Relations"). This prayer reminds us of our interconnectedness and to treat *all* life as sacred. It's a prayer I've been taught to live. We are also taught to take time regularly to hear our soul's nature and then act in accordance with that unique nature. This may be the singular most important thing for you to pay attention to. In the Western world, we are not taught to give the soul its due. Logistics take priority. Learning spirituality is not living as such. We have a collective belief that if we do our rituals and ceremonies, attend church, read the Torah, and recite prayers and quotes, then our work is done. I don't think so! The work is in the practice of remembering who you are; living the truth that your mind contains the Divine you pray to. You *are* the prayer. And as a child of the Divine, you belong to me and I belong to you. We are family.

In the naming ceremony, people are named to represent their indigenous nature and are thus living in their authority to live and bring that nature, that beauty, to all they touch, whether in thought, word, or deed. The Named One *is* the prayer. Others may not even know the name of a person who has undergone this profound ceremony, but they know who this person is by the way they walk in the world. When you are named, you don't need to rebel against the world and its stories any more than you have to comply. When you are named, you live the power of that naming by being in integrity with yourself.

This is not work; it's the framework of joy and freedom. Every indigenous culture has named what is sacred. We are all indigenous to this earth. This is not about having you adopt a Native American name or copy an indigenous practice. This is about you being rooted in your indigenous nature. The alive nature of your soul. This is the way of love. Knowing who you are without hesitation allows for a more centered, loving, and generative experience in the world. Isn't that what we want—a bit more confidence, a bit less self-doubt, less negotiation of our soul, and more alignment with our soul?

I've carried these naming ways into my coaching practice, where I've named entrepreneurs to be in alignment with their highest nature—their soul. Naming ended the negotiation of their work and stopped the compromising of their identity. It is a painful thing to not do the work you are here to do or to attempt to do it but never give yourself to it fully. It is painful not to live in your name and honor your gifts in this beautiful universe. It's equally painful to pretend you do not know your soul's nature and to take direction from anyone or anything that doesn't want to hear this nature sung into the world. In naming these entrepreneurs, we honored their souls' proper place in their business. When they could answer the question "Who are you?" unabashedly, they were free to do their work in integrity and on purpose. The mental struggles we have with ourselves keep us from truly being free. We are constantly going back and forth in our mind, discussing who we are and then striking that knowing down. When you believe what you long for in yourself, most of your suffering will be complete.

Misnaming will cause you to struggle. *Struggle* means to be held in restraint and to have difficulty coping.

Struggle is an unwillingness to hear the conversation of the soul. *Naming* is alignment. It is a life of congruence. It is living the prayer instead of constantly praying, longing, and wishing for it. Do you ever do a version of this? Find yourself misnamed by the story of your situation and just decide to live in it and from it? I hope you're bored by those conversations and those directives. The conversation we are seeking today is kinder and fiercely loyal to Self. It is true, but it needs you to hear it, to speak its truth, and then to own it. This is the conversation of admitting who you are.

As you turn the pages, you are walking into a ceremony. Make this your sacred time. Read, digest, and do your practices fully aware, without rushing. Be as present as you can. Do the work with like-minded people and be supported. Your walk in the world is about to get more intentional, more joyous, and more beautiful.

Melanie DewBerry
Ahe, Mitakuye Oyasin

Chapter 1

WHO ARE YOU, REALLY?

Who are you, really? This is the central question. The question you might have been asking yourself all these years. Who are you, without your title, your gender, your talent, your weight, your income, or your personality? If you strip away all your niceties, all the embellishments that you've added to your persona to be accepted, what is left? If you wriggle out of all the identities that others have foisted on you, if you release all the ways you smooth out your rough edges so you can belong and feel safe, who are you? What is your core identity?

And here is where most of us stumble. You can't answer this question with your analytical mind. The mind is susceptible to offering residence to your ego. Your mind holds two voices: the voice of the soul and the voice of the ego. The linear ego mind serves at the pleasure of data, labels, and roles. Its function is to sort information, judge this information, and put it in the appropriate box. It creates self-doubt, second-guessing, jealousy, and envy, just to name a few. Those qualities are accompanied by a host of behaviors. Just when you realize you are off-balance, the ego plays its trump card—justification—that loops you back into self-deception. The question of who you

1

are belongs to your soul, and you'll know if it's answering (or letting your mind/ego take over) by the texture of the reply. The soul's response will have the texture of relief. The ego wants you to be employed; the soul wants you to be at peace.

As you move through this chapter, you will be identifying the ways you protect yourself from your own self-knowing. You will learn the four ways we protect ourselves. This work will be confronting because lies and protections have made it so. It will be challenging to lay down your protections, because you have forgotten what safety really is, yet moving forward into the unknown is the path this work will take you on. Challenge the value you've given your protection for the values you want to live. You will be asked to take action in the practice at the end of the chapter. This is where you'll begin to identify the reason you cannot hear your name. You may find that you hold one or more protections as a means of creating a false sense of safety. In awareness, evolution has an opportunity to move you beyond the masks and shields that hide you.

You Are Not Who You Think You Are

You are *not* a lot of who you have been told you are. Trust me. There is a distinction to be made between the roles you play and who you truly are. The roles you play, like being a parent or an executive, the older sister or the peacemaker, are not the soul's definition of who you are. They are not your name. Nor are the labels "poor," "smart," "sexy," "fat," "black," "Latino," "immigrant," "male," or "female." Roles and labels attempt to tell your story, when in reality they are a narrow accounting of you, not the full measure of you. You are not your history—those

2

things that have occurred in your life so far—though you navigate the world based on memories and incidents. Yes, we make navigation a ritual of what we will or will not do or become, but the past is not your vision for you. You are not to be manicured by the events of your life. That is why, even with all the information of labels, data, history, and the roles we play, we still walk around feeling incomplete.

In order to walk on both feet, proud and alive in who you are, something has to die.

The Death of Personality

On the first rainy day of the year, I was sitting in a gorgeous wooden home in the hills of Santa Cruz, California, attending a writing workshop. In an intimate circle of eight people gathered in front of a fireplace, another writer, Dorothy, asked me to describe the process of naming to her.

"It's like holding the hands of someone dying. Have you done that?" I asked.

Yes, she nodded.

"You know that moment when you're holding their hands and you are savoring this moment of life between the two of you. There is the feeling that something holy is taking place, a communion of souls. I know that sounds strange and maybe scary, but the truth is we are not present to how precious and brief our life is, or how to live in our life. Until a death, either metaphorical or literal, we *do* ourselves into being. That's a strange sentence." I laughed. "Here's what I'm trying to say, Dorothy. Until death slides up to introduce itself, we don't recognize or remember our own divinity. We become what we learned in school, what our parents want, what our gender tells us, or we rebel

3

against all those things. But even as the rebel, we can get locked into the fight and not the journey of remembering. Death for some of my clients has looked like divorce, cancer, taking care of a dying parent, or losing a long-held career. Sometimes it's just learning to say no to those situations and people who are the bringers of death. In a morose but necessary way, death held their hands into the remembering of what is next. It helped answer the central question: Who are you, really?"

When you are named, you accept the status of the death of personality as your lead. Your data, your personality, and your ego were never meant to lead. As you move through this work, you come to understand that in being named you take a stand for your life, and life in total. You begin to see the beauty in your soul's story. You put down the artificial sacrifice to walk on a more sacred path. I once came upon a street sign on a country road that read: Pavement ends here. The Named One lives at the start of the unpaved road. It is entering new territory where life is organically wild but also in harmony and ever-changing; birth, death, and growth. Nature understands and surrenders to dying for the new to come forward. I know that sounds very profound and significant and it is both these things but in a very humble and grounding way. Naming is grounded in you remembering why you are here and who you are with an unapologetic and graceful knowing. You are with your name, your purpose, your path, because you know you need it. Without your name, anyone else, anything else, can and will write your life for you.

The only fight you ever need to take is the fight to live as you were created.

You Are Holy, Born to Dare

When you pretend you aren't who you are, a holy creation of divinity, you are dying. Period. It may not feel like death, but what do you think unhappiness and self-doubt are, if not death? If you do not rise each morning with the gratitude that joy of living in congruence with your soul brings, then you are distanced from your soul. Any confusion you have about walking the soul path of being named is a confusion that is externally prompted and internally accepted as a false truth. Remember, divine truth is the bringer of peace. This is the good news. You are not internally confused. The soul is housed in clarity. Confusion happens to the mind for three reasons.

The first is that we live in a world of loud messaging: "Follow me and my thinking. You don't need to think for yourself." The messaging is so pronounced and comes from so many corners that it is easy to believe what gets in the most as right and true. It removes us from soul ownership and keeps us in compliance. We are taught early in our lives that it is safer to let someone or something think for us than it is to risk thinking for ourselves. This kind of instruction also comes with the consequence of abandonment should you consider the brave move of listening to your own thinking.

The second way confusion gets in is when we don't create consistent time for soul connection—for the sensual connection with nature. When we do not quiet ourselves to hear the song of the universe. When we make no time to notice what has true resonance and dissonance, which makes us a tabula rasa for any graffiti our ego or the ego of others wants to scribble upon us. When we make no real time for listening to the god within. We may recite mantras, scriptures, and prayers, but they are never truly integrated.

We quote, but we do not humble our mind to the very recital coming from our lips. We do not truly believe we are one with God. We believe God is something we pray to for relief rather than knowing that our godliness is within, as is our relief. You are God, Goddess, Mother Earth.

The third reason confusion takes hold is predicated on the first two, and in the end makes us pregnant with our own unwillingness to be clear. The moment we begin to second-guess ourselves and compare ourselves to another, confusion has access to every inch of us and soon we are carrying its voice. *Confusion is vertigo to the soul.* It spins us, carefully, slowly at first, to sneak past our noticing.

However, when you are centered in your soul, when you are attending to the love of yourself, not much will get past you. In naming you are on a soul-chartered path that is unknown to anyone but you. (Sometimes it's even unknown to you!) Frankly, if you were to know what was ahead, you might not go. Your ego would mismanage this information and send up false flares. Walking with and listening to your name consistently reveals in each day, each moment, the next step after you've taken the one before it. In your name, courage will be emitted, faith followed, and risk-taking encouraged.

The power of naming begins to articulate you to you. You have a new way of speaking of yourself that is in alignment with your soul and thus new ways of being. It is a "re-languaging" of your reality to morph itself to accommodate this new you, this new vow. It's as though you decided to take up landscaping the most beautiful field called *you*.

The Challenge to Become You

Answering the question of who you are will bring you peace, but first it will also challenge you. It will dare you to speak your name. It will require you to live your name. The challenge for you is to answer the inquiry without force, caution, or denial; to dare to know your name.

How do you want to experience yourself in this lifetime? Why?

Yes, justify it. Justify it so you can hear your own yearning and desires, so you can hear your clarity. Defend yourself against the parts of you that don't want to die down but are killing your soul knowing. When this process of naming challenges you further, you'll need something with roots to hold on to as your false landscape falls away. Stay curious about your desires for yourself. Your life is not meant to be rote or routine.

Why do you want to be who you are?

Why are you needed in the world?

Why should you listen to your own truth?

What has your soul been saying to you that you unabashedly, unapologetically, unedited know to be true?

Who do you want to know yourself as?

What is your truth?

What is so compelling about your existence that the world would be remiss not to experience it?

No disclaimers. Resist the urge to soften or over-speak it. Take your time and answer completely. No wordsmithing. Don't try to find words that someone else will understand. Don't try to get it right. Just write.

Your answers are the representatives of your name. Those who are named serve the world by being who they genuinely are. There is nothing arrogant about naming your truth. Be of service; tell yourself who you are.

7

Breathe; you can be this divine you, because you already are.
I was working with a client living in Malaysia who longed to live in Paris but wouldn't give it to herself. Her interior self wanted to seed a new experience of herself. Isn't this true for all of us? We want something, but then our ego takes over and tells us how ridiculous it is. It defends its employment with brilliant accusations and calls in its close family member, *reason*. How many ways have you been told that what you desire is silly or that you can't leave the job, the marriage, the life you've built? Or that your job and life are great, that the money won't follow, that love won't find you? Your ego tells you that your life is safe as it is, and therefore it's best to stay put and forgo the unknown, which will surely leave you as a bag lady. Before you can really let yourself envision your new world, you heed the warning and douse the fire of your desires.

I urged my client to head in the direction of the nonsensical and host a moving-to-Paris party. She needed to peel it all back to see what was true for her, to strip off the wallpaper to see the beauty of what was painted beneath.

I asked my client, "What wants to be free to build great roots for your next you? What do you want to give yourself that you are ignoring?" This was my way of asking, Who are you, really? She was an artist who hadn't touched her art in years. It wasn't even stored in her home. She literally and spiritually lived apart from her art.

Is your art at home with you? Is it living, breathing, growing, and evolving in the home of your soul? We live in a world that favors resistance and discipline: "Resist those urges and they will go away." But that is never true. Yes, you might bury your art, your passion, but those unfulfilled aspects of your nature live in you, causing you suffering and despair. It's like being thirsty and not giving yourself water. Urges are not whimsy; they are the first voice of a calling. They are passion. Urges are advocating for you to exist. Urges are the god within speaking directly to you.

The Story Becomes You: Francisco's Story

It's 97 degrees in the desert of Gallup, New Mexico. We are all camping on a beautiful Diné (Navajo) reservation in attendance of the Sundance Ceremony. When it's hot like it is now and the dancers and drummers are taking a break, it's time to do nothing else but hear the stories since our last gathering, laugh, and play games. There is something about this land that calls forth confessions of mind and conflicts of soul. The rez (Indian reservation) has a way of exfoliating old skin. When we return home to our life it is never business as usual. We return with rumblings of transformation. We have left our conflicts of who we are and what we are to do in the desert of this holy land. There, what wasn't useful will be repurposed into the land. What we take with us is a new story that becomes our life.

Francisco swirls his coffee, looking at it with trepidation.

"What, is the coffee not good?" I ask.

"No, I was just thinking," he says as he continues to stare downward.

"Well, think out loud, I need to be entertained," I say, thinking maybe I can lighten the mood.

Without hesitation he lets it spill. "I've gotta make a presentation to a group of high school teachers about how to reach our children. They've had long careers and they just aren't engaged the way the kids need them to be, the way I know they want to be, and I don't know how to say what I want to say."

"Keep talking, Francisco. It's coming out right now. Keep talking."

"I could talk to them about the students' needs, about their values and impact, but . . ."

Silence stretches its arms to give him the space he needs.

"But what I really want to tell them is, what I really want to say is, to *love* them. Love the children. They have to love the children."

There you have it. His knowing. Who he is. Francisco is a man within a school system who wants teachers to love the children. He wants them to remember why they began teaching. They have to love the children to reach them.

Within the school system and other bureaucracies, the word *love* will raise eyebrows. Francisco could have been tempted to negotiate the language of love into words like *leadership* or *mission* in an attempt to sound relevant and pacify his ego. He could have given in to the call of confusion. Instead, there in the heat of the desert, Francisco answered the call within. He spoke to his knowing, his message, and his love. Maybe it was being in the providence of the reservation, of all that is holy and sacred, that wouldn't allow him to dismiss himself.

I've been Francisco. You have, too—so close to your truth, but so unsure that it will be heard and accepted. We contemplate negotiating the language of the soul to hush the demands of fear. What if he did say "love" and it did not register to the teachers? He would receive feedback. He would know if he's in his right work. He could find out when the teachers loved their work and their children. He could help them remember.

In the desert, Francisco saw clearly how he was attempting to deny what was true. He felt the push toward dissonance rather than the pull toward resonance. He dared himself to speak resonance.

I said to him, "Love isn't vague, nor should be what you say to them. Help them see what the power of love in the context of school could look like. Don't worry about what they'll think of you. Focus on the impact that speaking your truth will make. Trust this conversation."

If you say "I cannot be who I am," then that is who you will be. That is the life you will experience. You are already naming yourself. But is it a powerful name? Is it a true name? Is it congruent naming? Whoever you are now is a name, and who you name yourself to be is what you behave into the world. Discredit, disclaim, or negate who you are, and we will accept that as the truth as well. Own who you are, your luscious presence, your knowing, and your voice, and we will accept this as truth.

Whatever you believe about yourself, so shall we.

The Four Ways of Protection

Review the ways you try to protect yourself by asking yourself these questions. Gaining a deeper understanding of your patterns and your personality will help you complete the practice at the end of the chapter.

Are You the Rebel with the Sword?

Are you the angry one? The one who fights to be visible but slays everything on the path? The activist who uses

11

only anger rather than compassion to be heard? Believing that anger is really power but not feeling powerful in the world? Believing your anger is justified? After all, life has not been fair to you, right? This is true for many of us. Life hasn't been fair. How about reaching for something higher than fairness? How about letting go of the sword to see what wants to be embraced within you that will give you something better than fair? Isn't it time for you to be fully seen and heard without the slaying of others? Aren't you a little curious to see how you can be respected, validated, and needed without having to work every muscle so hard? What are your assumptions about being invisible that the sword in your hand speaks to? Are you so angry at the injustices of life that you believe you are not heard if you are not angry? Are you putting up fences and slicing anyone who shows you kindness because you are suspicious of their intentions? How can they be kind without wanting something?

Anger has an imperative: to be heard. We can easily see where our value is being stepped on through the eyes of anger, but anger is not the end of the path. If all you have is anger, all you get is a self-made prison. Anger has relevance when it leads you to resolution, especially when the resolution is within. When the ego joins with anger, it will tell you that without external resolution from others, you have given up; you are weak. The ego wants you to stay in prison. A prison of anger, of fear, embitterment, it makes no difference to the ego, prison is prison. Have bad things happened to you? Yes. But staying angry keeps the ghost of yesterday haunting your life today. How do you want to resolve your anger? Being offended can become your air. It's so easy to look outside yourself for resolution because you believe the problems started out there. If I waited for others to make me free as a black woman I would still be waiting. All the laws and policies, all the toleration teachings we made in this world are not the only antidote to me feeling safe and loved. This is my work to do, just as your work is yours to do.

When you put down the sword, you can master any part of your life. Each time you choose to grip the sword, you lose your grip on a reality of love. You cannot simultaneously hold the sword and be embraced by life. Life takes a conscious choosing to be lived in love. Anger doesn't hide the fact that you want to be seen and loved for who you are and yet you fear it. Don't you want to be loved and seen for all you are? What does your anger believe it can do that love can't? Whatever the reply, send the answer back to whatever closed mind it came. You don't have to live there anymore. Whatever your justifications for anger, it is not the true accounting of you. Anger doesn't know you the way love does. Anger doesn't want you to be unprotected and safe. Anger doesn't want you to know how powerful you are without it. Anger is lost in its own cyclical mess of believing that safety and love cannot coexist. You were created with a wealth of diverse emotions to keep you dynamic in your evolution.

Are You the Masked One?

Are you the one who won't show us who you really are because in truth, you don't know who you really are? Have you lived behind this mask for so long that you've almost forgotten your raw beauty? Somewhere, someone told you not to be you. Maybe what hindered you were your circumstances or your data—poverty, wealth, weight, sexual preference, or gender. Somewhere you got the very clear message that you were not quite right simply being you, you were not good enough, and you heeded that message as your truth. So you masked your soul with niceties, manipulations, passiveness, managing, and controlling. Are you the 40-year-old woman who giggles after every comment so you don't threaten anyone? Do you say you're sorry for the slightest received indiscretions so you will be liked? Are you afraid to really be seen— never letting us see who you are because we may not like what we see? Are you being a chameleon wherever you go? Pretending to have it all together? Or worse, are you making constant comparisons with others and never quite measuring up? Oh, the many ways we mask ourselves, afraid that the world will hurt us if we take off our masks.

Always being nice, are you? Because if you're nice and don't say no then we have to like you? Because being nice is expected? What is the exchange rate on nice? What does it cost for you to not be who you really are? What bargain-basement trade are you making with nice? Every nice act is asking for validation and acceptance. How afraid are you of your real gifts? What story do you make up that keeps them locked away? How well versed are you in defending your fear that it has become the only voice you now hear? The Masked One's prison is one of passive-aggressiveness. Always manipulating reality to bend to them. All with such a nice smile. Genuine kindness doesn't ask for anything in return. It doesn't have pretense. It's generous for generosity's sake. Being a good "fill in blank"—mother, son, teacher, Christian, spiritual person, father—is not measured by disingenuous niceties. Every time you are being nice, you tell your fear it has the power to own you.

Maybe you are the Masked One who has it all together. You could charm a room. Or perhaps you're the smart one with all the answers, always finding a way to be relevant so you are appreciated and valued. You studied and got all those acronyms behind your name to prove your worth. Your beauty opens doors, but will they stay open once you are seen? What happens when you can't answer, or you don't know, or we stop being interested in your input or your looks? What happens when we stop believing your particular masquerade? Is your mask the person who tries to get it right? Say the right thing, be in the right place, show that you are present but in truth you're present to the longing of validation. Whatever your pattern, the Masked One is always full of anxiety. Stillness isn't part of your being behind the mask. Your hustle is constant. No one really gets all of you. What talents and what loves do you have that you don't touch or won't tell others about? Who would you see if you ripped that mask off? What could you count on from yourself if you came clean? What relief will you have when the mask has no purpose?

Are You the Shielded One?

Are you the strong one with a capital S? People look to you for answers but you never let them in, do you? You are the tough one who commands life. Some look up to you as a leader, but you never let them see your vulnerability. Your command is so strong that it puts up fences and few are allowed entry. Even those who gain entry are patted down for weapons of vulnerability and kept at arm's length.

Are you the older brother who steps in and cares for the siblings, paying their bills, taking care of their children, working long hours because you can? You believe you can and they cannot. Perhaps you are the parent who cares and loves for the child alone though your spouse lives with you. She cannot give like you, so you do it all, full of pride as you complain to friends about her lack of parenting skills. It's all on your shoulders. After all, you are the "strong one." But each time you wear the mask of the strong one you emasculate others around you by silently telling them they cannot take care of themselves. You cannot know yourself unless you're carrying their water for them. It is safer to be tough than it is to be truly strong.

Are you the smart one, the humorist who deflects closeness by upping the intelligence quota or spinning funny stories that no one can equal? Each time you don the mask of the strong one you tell yourself it's your strength, your intelligence, your humor that covers you with safety, but your soul knows it only offers distance.

Are you the stubborn one who won't budge and defends her fear with intelligence and logic? Each defense keeps you locked in a fortress of your own making. Nothing new gets in and you don't get out. Your mask keeps you stuck. You're brilliant in reality. Your art is so illuminating it scares you. You see its beauty but you won't consistently honor it with integrity. Your fear of being seen is large but not as large as your luminous soul. Come out of your dark closet. The thing about closets is that their sole purpose is storage.

If you allowed vulnerability—one of the cornerstones of being named—to seep into you, you'd let others see how tired you are. We would also see how scared you are and how fragile you really are. Instead, you walk around with armor, refusing to let us in. How many times have you heard that the world needs you to be more vulnerable or that people want to get to know you better? Protecting some old wound with that wall, are you? You are deeply sensitive and kind, but we have to work hard to feel loved by you. Is *hard* what you show first? Hesitating on the very thing that would bring you joy because then we'd see you? You are hiding, but not from us; you are hiding from what you fear. What good could happen if you put down your guard? What is tender in you that we will see when you let us in? And, what story do you make up about our seeing you fully that keeps you shielded?

Are You the Island One?

Are you the one who is always fine? You're in deep physical pain, but no matter, no one needs to know, and when you are asked, you parrot the standard "I'm fine." You are in financial woes, but you're fine. Your marriage is falling apart, but you're fine. You're lonely and wonder if love will ever come, but you're fine. Your child is in trouble with the law, but you're fine. Your parent died, but you're fine. People say about you, "If Stuart is upset, then it must be bad." "If Caroline is crying, then you know something awful has happened." And that validates you, doesn't it? Emotions are something weak people express. *Handle it yourself,* your internal voice repeats. You walk around with a smile that hides your inner world. You tell yourself you are not a complainer and that keeps you locked in "I'm fine," because honesty, and pulling pack the veil, could be construed as complaining, being a downer, or being weak. You are logical and rational. When someone else shares a hard time, you put a positive spin on it and inwardly you think they are weak. Or you turn it around to make it sound better and bring the brighter side. There is a way to be in the world, right? Suck it up. Do what has to be done. If you don't like it, well, that is life, isn't it? Pretense has

17

moved you to a remote island where compassion, caring, generosity, and unconditional love cannot visit you.

We each get scared into our swords, masks, shields, or islands. My final question for you is this: Who are you *without* these defenses? How much energy are you using to make others believe you? Your energy is needed elsewhere. It's time to go within. What is the truth asking of you that scares you so? You're going to have to put your guard down to hear the answers that will support your awakening. Drop the facades. It's not really working for you anyway. You can't hold the doors shut and reach for an opening at the same time.

Don't wait one more moment to be free. Who are you, really?

The Practice: The Laying Down of False Protections

This is the first of many practices you will encounter in this book. Get your journal and a pen. Feel the texture of these pages beneath your fingers. This is your first retraining: getting in the habit of keeping notes. There is power in writing. The pen etching against the paper reveals your wisdom. The other reason to scribe yourself into becoming is that when you forget what you've accomplished—when you return to old haunts of yourself that chase you down the rabbit hole of *no, not me, I can't*—you will have a record of *yes, I can; yes, I want this*, and all the other truths you've etched on the page. If you like the digital world, you can use that format, though I encourage pen and paper because the tactile experience of feeling the pen against the paper provides a visceral recording of your truths that typing cannot witness.

With each practice I encourage you to slow your pace down to a crawl. In a very real sense, there is nothing to do but be present. When taking a stroll in nature, you take time to marvel at it, listening to it speak into you. It is the same with these practices. Slow down. Don't let fear tell you to speed through this because it's hard to be with. Uncovering your name is the beginning of yet another leg of the journey of you. Let go of wanting the experience or the results. Think of each practice as a sacred act, like giving a newborn a bath. Touch into each moment. Allow your senses to brighten. When the practice is complete, take additional time to breathe. Give yourself and the practice space to process. Resist the urge to go on to the next event in your life for a few minutes.

In this practice you are going to lay down your sword, your mask, or your shield and leave your island. You're going to have to lay them down to hold space for your forthcoming name. It may be helpful to read the instructions first and to record them on your phone and play them back. That way you can be fully present to the practice.

Time: minimum of 30 minutes
Materials: journal and pen

Plant your feet on the floor and loosen your body. Breathe.

Relax your chin and your jaw. Breathe and drop your shoulders.

Breathe and relax your legs and feet.

Close your eyes and in your mind's eye see roots growing from the soles of your feet down into the earth. Deeper and deeper.

Mother Earth has got you. She's holding you.
Feel your beauty. Your richly textured self.
Bow your head to this beauty and write from this place.
Practice trusting your internal voice. You're going to fall in love with that voice.

Breathe and respond in wholehearted vulnerability and raw truth.

1. The ways in which I have hidden myself in the past are _____

2. What I want others to see in me is _____

3. I am tired of fearing _____

4. The price I pay in hiding, in avoiding, is _____

5. I am missing out on knowing and experiencing _____

6. The help I need from others that I've never asked for is _____

7. My age/weight/gender/culture (fill in the blank) have caused me to protect and hide myself because _____. I want to be accepted as _____

8. Who I really am is (use every adjective and verb that is true) _____

9. What I'm ready to admit about who I want to be and the life I want to live is _____

10. I want to know my name because _____

11. What I know I am here to do is _____

12. What I'm ready to experience is _____

13. What I want people to experience/see/count on me for that is different from what they have seen before is _____
_____

Breathe. Breathe this life, this you, in deeply.

It takes time for the truth to drop down. Take at least a couple of turns at this work and then ask yourself, What else? "What else?" is an incredibly powerful question. Answer it until it is all spilled out. You will know when you are finished because you will begin repeating yourself.

When you are done, take three deep breaths. End your practice with a ritual that you will continue for all the practice sessions to come. You can say "Amen," you can offer up a prayer of gratitude, or bow to yourself. You can say out loud, "I am willing to be the Named One." Whatever you choose remember to honor yourself for walking on this road. It may not always be easy, but it is good. Drink some water. Water of life.

P.S. You may have dreams that speak more truth to you. Nighttime is a window of opportunity for the soul to speak without obstruction. Keep your notebook close to you when you sleep to record anything. Trust me, you won't remember in an hour or when you wake.

Chapter 2

SACRED LISTENING

There is an important distinction to be made between listening and hearing. Listening is the power of presence. Listening is not simply what you hear with your ears or the ability to tell someone verbatim what they said without listening to what they meant. Listening is a full-body experience. When you listen you are holding another in grace. Intuition is present and replaces that ungrounded feeling of having to be prepared with responses and rebuttals. Listening extends a net of safety and care. Listening is love.

Hearing automatically creates distance. There is *you* and there is *me* and we are separate: I hear your words as they relate to me and my experiences. We validate what we hear if it matches what we believe, and thus we judge and lock out anything that doesn't match our experiences. Hearing is riddled with assumptions. You believe you're listening but you're interpreting what you heard based on your experiences rather than listening without reference. I call this the "archived presence." In an archived presence you are filtering the world through your past experiences in order to discern safety. *Am I safe?* is the first filter.

Most archives are based on hurt and interruptions from the past. Someone says something in current time and you get angry because you hear it from a pain of years gone by. Someone says they love you and you drop your boundaries, because the desperation to be loved in the way you were not in your younger years "hears" for you and responds. Most of us are in a constant state of preparing our responses to defend the archive. A person speaks to us on a difficult topic and we run all that is said through our defense filter. We think we are protecting ourselves but we are only defending and keeping in place the interruptions of the past.

When we hear what is being said from our wounds, we make decisions out of hurt, anger, desperation, and fear. We are in reaction mode, creating our present moments out of the wounds of the past. And we wonder why we don't have the consistent and sustainable experiences we dream of. We are so tuned in to yesterday that we block the voice within telling us who we really are right now. We misplace the integrity of listening with the defended stance of hearing. The truth shouldn't have to swim upstream to get to us.

Listening doesn't engage filters because it has no need for them. When you listen you are simply present with what is being said. What is said gets in, rather than being served back to the speaker with your filtered spin on it. Listening is an art that you will learn how to practice. You will listen to the world with fresh ears because this beautiful world is giving you insights, directives, and hope for what will come. Releasing yourself to listen well prepares you for the deeper soul conversations that your inner self is having with you.

When I was growing up my filters of protection around racism were busy sifting the words of others through the lens of "What harm do they intend to wield?" and "What offense are they about to make?" No wonder so many people of color are exhausted before they even enter adulthood! At 18, the core conversation between my friends and me was how tired we were of being in a world that hurts. Pain wants healing, not scenario-building and defensive listening. It takes an incredible amount of energy to fore-think everything. All the isms of the world are real and change and growth don't happen from protection.

Recall when you had to have a serious conversation how many scenarios you ran through your mind about what you would say if the other person said X. Or what you would do if the other person didn't do X. So many of us are creating scenarios and responses to scenarios that have never occurred and will never occur. Our beautiful brains are wasting our art on the deception and defensiveness of scenario-making.

As you practice listening in each hour and each day, your awareness of what serves you will become a natural act. The scenario-making falls away like dead skin, replaced by visioning and living a more self-loving reality, even in the face of isms. This work does not deny the very real pain and hurt that go on in the world. This work holds the space for the dignity of love.

In this chapter you will rewire the hearing of the past to a deep and profound experience of listening in the present. You will stop creating your life from yesteryear. Instead, you will have the ability to address and meet those longings and needs, and you will move into the now. You will give yourself an authentic and engaged experience with life, rather than a predetermined one from long ago.

Listening, like all the work you will do in this book, asks you to let go of your association with the false protections you unearthed in the first chapter. Listen for the love of yourself and others. You will easily move into what life is giving you now and how joyously abundant it is. You will experience how safe it feels to be you, and how being you is the only protection you ever needed. When pain comes forward, you will hear the purpose of pain and how to move with it. Thoughts of lack and the compulsion to compare yourself to others will be eradicated by the sensual attraction of the sounds of truth, connection, and freedom. Do you think you do not know your name? It can only be so because the daring space of listening has not been given its due.

The Radical Power of Listening

Listening is a provocative way of cultivating courage and bravery. This way of being opens the door for vulnerability to enter your life. Vulnerability will show you the strength and serenity that dwells within. This strength is quiet. It has nothing to prove. It quietly clears the overgrown weeds of fear. That may not sound important but in reality we can't change what we don't know about.

When we are truly present and listening—to another or to ourselves—we enter a sacred space. It is sacred to catch with your heart and with your soul the intimacy that someone is offering you. They are offering you a guided tour of *their* heart and soul. They are offering you a seat in their sorrows, their desires, and their dreams. It is an act of grace to be deeply embraced by another's presence. Remember the last time you were held by another—that amazing experience when you didn't even notice what was happening around you because you were so engaged in the moment? You didn't hear the sirens as they passed by, or the other conversations around you. Moments like this happen in the aisle of the grocery store as easily as in the arms of your child or lover. This is the embrace of listening that you will live into more and more.

The Intimacy of Listening to Self

You can easily and always hear the ramblings of your crazy mind. The ego is constantly spinning itself. But to hear your *soul* takes courage. No one evolves without being able to converse with their spirit, the spiritual world, and the girth of their soul's voice. When you are able listen to your own sorrows, desires, insecurities, and longings, and to do so with compassion, you will already be sitting in the seat of peace.

We have been taught to run from what is soft and tender. It has been called weakness. It has been ridiculed. But all that is tender is also gracious, kind, and loving. The soft skills are the hardest to attain. But aren't they integral to the reality you want to be a part of? Surrendering to your vulnerability, your soft interior, and then giving it life is where the poetry of life is rooted. It's tender there, and when you live from this place you open yourself up to the possibility of being hurt. That's the fear, isn't it—to be hurt? But the truth is that even with your mask and your shield and your sword, even as you remain on your island, the hurts pile up. How can it be otherwise if you are still filtering all your life experience through the archives?

To evolve and walk in your name, the soft underbelly of yourself must be available to you. True bravery is a humbling approach to life because the consistent act of listening to and acting on your divine mandate challenges everything you think you know about yourself. You begin to understand that trust begins with trusting your own voice, your own truth, and your own visions. The strength of your power is in direct relation to how connected you are to your ability to be vulnerable. Listening to the call to your own life will give you clear sight and perspective of what is needed from you. Most of us live in the hindsight paradigm. We can only see afterward, when we've untied ourselves from the grip of yesterday's hold.

Resting Your Resistance

Listening happens in the space of surrender. Surrendering means to stop resisting. All those interruptions built a barrier that cemented you in resistance to your own inner beauty, to your own voice. The act of surrender is being willing to hear yourself without editing. It is a surrendering to the faith that you were designed in absolute perfection to work in harmony with this delicious universe.

Surrender means to let go of any fortresses or fences that keep you from yourself and others. It's not a free fall without a net. You are being held. Let go of the constructs you've depended on to hold you. There is rooting that must take place now.

Crying for Your Vision

In the Native traditions of the Red Road, ceremonies are one way in which we reconnect to Mother Earth. In this connection we remember that our essence is in concert with the essence of the earth. Ceremonies are our time to strip away anything that separates us from our inner nature and the nature of the earth. It is our time to honor this relationship and to intentionally stay in tune with nature, our wisest elder. One of those ceremonies is the vision quest, also called "crying for a vision" or "going on the hill." It is a ceremony to quiet yourself for a listening within to identify your purpose or your vision. The vision quest is a solo journey. We stay in one place to pray and sing. We are enclosed in a circle of prayer ties that hold us and protect us. During this four-day and four-night vigil, we are unobstructed by the day-to-day logistics of life. We eat no food and drink no water. There are no journals to write in, nor do we wander away from our sacred prayer circle. We sit and stand in prayer, listening to the conversation of the Creator within. This is our practice of surrender to the spirit. The spirit will only come when we've opened up to our most vulnerable point, allowing it to transform us with our deepest divine truth. I think of the vision quest as an ongoing conversation between my soul and the Creator. We are not praying up to the heavens or outside of ourselves. We are praying through our soul or consciousness to ourselves and to the Creator within. Our vision is given to us as it is heard within us. The Star Nation and nature that surrounds us join the conversation, giving us their updates and wisdom. It is our work to listen deeply to spirit in all its forms. Alone, on a hill, without distractions, it is our surrendered listening that allows us to hear the call that becomes the vision. It is the practice of living into the beauty within.

The Thunder Beings

On my third vision quest, I was put on a hill in the New Mexican desert where it can easily reach over 100 degrees. It was the third day of four. I was tired and I was very thirsty. As I sat praying for the fourth day to come more quickly, I heard something from afar. I turned to see if it was an animal or perhaps Uncle Pablo coming to check on me. In a flash I was approached by the Thunder Beings—beings hovering over my shoulders, in a bubble. They asked me to come with them to visit the two worlds I was living in. I agreed, and was transported into a large bubble. As we flew inside the bubble they asked me to look down and to take note of what I experienced. The first bubble was a world with war, hate, and crime. The air was gray as if buildings had fallen. Children were neglected and elders forgotten. We flew into a second bubble. I was given the same directions. As I flew over this world, it could not have been more different. It was green and luscious. There was love and harmony. Elders were sitting under apple trees teaching the young ones. I wanted to stay here but they said no. I was then brought back to the mountain I was sitting on. They asked me, "Which world do you want to belong to?" Thinking this was some kind of a joke, I laughed as I replied, "The world of beauty, of course." "Good," they said, "then go create it." And with that they were gone. I sat there so angry in my last day. How could I alone create a world of beauty from a world of chaos? "This is an impossible task!" I shouted into the air.

Months later when I was meditating at my home I heard a voice whisper in my ear: "We will send help." It would take me over a decade to realize that they were not asking me to change the world around me. They were instructing me to change my internal world from one of chaos to one of beauty. That is the work you and I are doing within the pages of this book. You are my help and I am yours.

When our elders prepare us for the vision quest, I have listened to them warn the men in particular who are "going on the hill," that toughening up will not help them. You cannot train to get strong for it, or drink enough water beforehand to avoid the thirst—I know, I tried. This journey is not about physical strength. It is not about endurance or about proving oneself by pushing through all four days. You can tough it out and stay for the four days but not really have been in a ceremony.

A true vision quest is a ceremony of deep humility. To sit and listen to your voice is incredibly humbling and vulnerable. The "hill" is our classroom and it is full of challenges to the masculine in all of us. To be quiet and still in your body and your mind is wrought with challenge in today's world where multitasking and working long hours is normal and expected. Going on the hill, in part, is done to reverse these messages and to reset our system to our organic nature that is naturally attuned to a higher vibration. We instinctually know there is a more resonant voice than the one we are taught to listen to in the larger society. Our dark nature, our truth, our desires, our intuition, our fears, all come forward when we are still and quiet. It takes time to surrender. Perhaps this is why we are given four days and four nights to do so. Each day we rise with the sun and feel a new opportunity to speak and listen to the wisdom of the Star Nation, Father Sky, Mother Moon, and the Creator within. Four days to feel how we are held by an expansive universe that wants us to truly live abundantly. Perhaps this is why when we commit to the vision quest we commit to doing it four times: once a year for four years.

In traditional Western society, we are not guided to stillness—to hear the wisdom of the trees or to stop long enough to listen within. When was the last time you had four days to be quiet, alone, without distraction, with support, all to hear your universal truth about who you are and why you are here? Your name, like all truths about you, lives within. Your quest requires your presence in stillness.

Your Quest

The journey to your spiritual identity is a quest. In your way you are crying for your vision. It is a time of deep listening to the voice within, without interruptions of your past. Listening means being curious. Listening to your truth can be both exhilarating and exhausting. It's exhilarating to hear the bounty of your beauty. At first it's exhausting to keep your fears in the corner. Just remember: Listening is love, and love is kind. Be kind with yourself.

Often when I return from a ceremony like the vision quest I sleep for 15 hours at time. I am between worlds, the one of spirit and the one of flesh. Stepping between worlds takes energy. Sleep gives my higher consciousness time to reassemble me in a way that my awake self has yet to learn. As you do each of the practices, take care of yourself. You too will be dancing between the spirit world and the world of flesh. Give yourself the space that becoming needs. Feed yourself well. Rest well and laugh often. Listening to your soul is a daring act. You are daring your ego to die. You are daring the desire in you to emerge and speak for itself. You are daring to be known. Your soul wants to know if you are willing to take this unknown journey, the journey into facing your fears and being freed from them. This is the journey of faith. Faith is walking toward your name without knowing much else. Faith coupled with fierce determination to know yourself fully is all you need. Hang tight in faith and determination when the exhaustion wants you to quit or when the ego tells you, "It's not happening."

When you do your to-do list and appointments, say "Get back to this quest another time." When the voice of guilt says, "Your child needs you and this is your only priority," know that the voice of *fear* is speaking. Recognize it now because fear has had many years to sharpen itself. Fear is clever, believable, logical, and rational, but those voices are not the truth. Truth never makes you feel guilty or has you second-guessing yourself. It may make you feel uncomfortable, but don't confuse that with guilt. Guilt is an ethical and immoral indicator. Discomfort is what we feel when we are learning to be in congruence with our soul. Truth will abolish the lie. Hold steadfast in it. You are now being guided by beauty. Beauty is the conversation that wants to emerge within you. It is carrying your name. It is daring you to live into what is true, compassionate, graceful, and loving. It is daring you to drop all the facades that you've mastered for the love and freedom you want and deserve. Who will accept you as this? your ego asks. But that is the wrong question. The ego always poses the wrong questions. The inquiry of the soul is: Will you have the courage to own and walk in your beauty?

The Practice

Part I: Be Present to Another by Listening

Choose your audience. Is it a child, an in-law, a co-worker, a neighbor, or a news channel? Choose someone you struggle to be present with because they annoy you, frustrate you, or perhaps they are just different from you. Find your way to this person with the purpose of crossing over to being present rather than planning your getaway. Start with the intention of leading with love. Love this person and listen. Humanize them. Look at them and find something to love—their eyelashes, for example. Though that seems superficial, it will lead to a profound realization. With intention you can love and stay present with anyone. Breathe in that this person is like you, wanting to be seen and loved as they are. Stay present for three minutes the first time, then five minutes, eventually moving up to ten full minutes. As you listen, find many things to love them for. They will feel you loving them. People will surprise you when you are present and in love. You will be surprised at who you can love.

This practice can be expanded to be present with a group, an idea, a political position you are not comfortable with, or a perspective that may unnerve you. You are asked here to offer this level of grace even when it may, at first, feel uncomfortable. Presence doesn't require you to agree or support another's ideals. It only asks you to honor another by being fully present. Imagine if this kind of grace hadn't been available to Dr. Martin Luther King, Jr. While there were many people committed to separation and racism, there were those who listened fully and heard in their bones the truth justice was speaking. Turn on the news to a channel you tend to resist. Read an article you wouldn't ordinarily because you assume you know the writer's view. Listen to a relative you've previously avoided. Listen to them, to what they are saying not only with their words but also with their energy and presence. Notice when you want to wander mentally. Notice your judgments and stay present; you don't have to agree. Notice what your body is doing with what is being said. What does that feeling in your body tell you? Let it go. Don't suppress it or turn it into something positive. Simply let it go. Once you recognize what it is doing in your body and how it forms your thinking, you can see how you resist the world around you and how others may resist your world. Surrender your judgments and your desire for it to be over.

Part II: Listening for Congruence

Time: 10 minutes every hour throughout your day
Materials: journal and pen

Now that you have moved from hearing to listening, you can be present to that which you do not align with. You have prepared yourself for a deeper listening, a listening for things that are in congruence with you. You have the capacity for both: listening for when it doesn't work for you, and listening for when it does. Congruence harmonizes you with the power of love. It's a vibration that carries you forward, giving you situations in which to cultivate wisdom and be groomed with grace.

Congruence conveys truth. The truth resides within your mind and your body, where you will now learn to deeply listen for it.

Start with listening to the body, as it is often the easier of the two to hear. Every thought and emotion you have has an experience in your body. For example, when I get angry, my throat gets warm. Anxiety gives me a stomachache. Once you start paying attention to the signals in your body, you can choose how to respond to give yourself the proper remedy. You will know you are in congruence because it feels resonant. It's like getting the thumbs-up in your body. Congruence is not seductive. It will not make you feel as though you are taken away to some decadent place that "feels" good but has a huge price tag attached to it. This is temptation. Congruence is alignment, but it does not necessarily mean that what is being asked of you is easily done in body. In fact, it is more easily completed by spirit.

Be still and listen throughout your day. When someone annoys you, how does it show up in your body?

If you have negotiated with yourself, how do you experience this?

Note what hurts you and what heals you. Which are you giving more of your attention to?

After you've done these short practices throughout the day, what do you want to change in your life or in your perception?

Chapter 3

CHILDHOOD INTERRUPTED

When you were a very young child, you knew your name. You embodied it, lived it. But at some point most of us suffered an interruption by an adult—by someone who was not present literally or emotionally, by someone who smothered us, limited us, and made the rules more important than we were. Some interruptions are traumatic events; others are seemingly innocent moments of carelessness by unconscious adults. Some interruptions arise out of the cultures we grow up in and the society around us. Other interruptions happen by chance or by appointment. Your parents, teachers, pastors, or family members say or do something that attempts to diminish you. Sadly, it's the nature of our human experience to be interrupted. Your grounding, your sense of self, your pure innocence, your unique magic and curiosity are halted or deleted by the unconscious moment of another. The suffering from interruptions can last a person's entire life. We tuck ourselves away, locking what was precious and pure away for safekeeping, and just like that, the beauty that was us becomes remote and hidden. While suffering is not something we raise our hands for, we all experience pain throughout our lives. While we cannot undo our pain, we can reclaim the aspects of our nature that were interrupted, rewriting them to be more subtle and beautiful than they were in our younger years.

Those who interrupt us are acting out of their own wounds. Imprisoned by their fear, taught to deny their beauty, disconnected from their soul name, they too were interrupted and are suffering. One way people deal with never being able to live their vision is to project their pain onto others. Many years ago, I was shivering with fear after a colleague told me I did not have the skills and ability to start a magazine. Hearing this, my friend Carla said to me: "Everyone has shit that they carry around with them. Most people are trying to get rid of it by putting it in your pocket.

"Your job," she told me, "is to keep your hands in your own pockets to keep that from happening." "What about my shit?" I asked. "Oh honey, turn it into fertilizer and grow your garden beautiful," she replied.

How much and how long you stay interrupted depends on your willingness and desire to remember who you are and face your pain and your glory.

Are You Attached to Your Old Story?

A person on pause becomes busy with managing the hurts of their story of being interrupted. Everything they do today is in response to the past. They tell the story of their wounds to anyone who will listen, not realizing that with each retelling they keep themselves stuck in a cycle of pain of their own making. Telling your story once or twice is freeing. More than that and it becomes your legacy. You cannot split your focus between managing your pain and answering the call of the one who will be named. The soul cannot be attended to with partial focus. It's an all-in conversation.

When your life is stunted by childhood interruptions, your intimate connection to your soul is also put on pause. It is within this intimate place, within your soul, that you are told about your Original Story and your Original Medicine. When you are interrupted, the loving whispers of your divine guide are knocked out of ear range, or are only partially heard, perhaps misheard. The pain of interruption ends when you can stop resisting it, when you quit throwing mantras and affirmations on top of your pain, when you quit arranging your world so as not to bump into all that is put on pause. Your positive talk, mantras, and quotes have real medicinal properties, but they have to enter deep within: where they are not Band-Aids or quick fixes. You cannot slather a mantra on top of years of suffering, but you can stop the interruptions and get on with the wild and harmonic adventure that awaits the one who will be named.

Now that you are no longer that child who could not take a stand for him- or herself, you sit in the seat of control. You can be with the pain without being defined by it. When you can sit in the pain of being interrupted without needing to flee or change it, you can then walk away and shut that door forever, or incorporate what needs to be incorporated and move forward. And while pain and suffering will visit again in your lifetime, you will not be held prisoner by it.

A Case for Compassion

Though suffering and pain are challenging, they can guide each of us to a gentler way of being with each other, and hopefully with ourselves, too. The experience of suffering, when fully understood, is one of the oldest teachers of compassion. Compassion for yourself is critical, especially as you move toward transformation. Adults do not like learning curves. We think that we should be able to hit the ground running. But the truth is that on this journey we will fall and fall again before we walk. As you move toward the unveiling of your name, as you unlearn some of the pain, you will need to hold tight to compassion.

Compassion escorts trust and tenderness into our life because we are often our own worst enemy, in part due to the interruptions we encountered. One of the by-products of being interrupted is the tendency to second-guess ourselves and to doubt our ability to take care of ourselves by speaking up, saying no, and establishing healthy boundaries. Compassion does not deny our mistakes nor our responsibility for the ways we might have impacted the lives of others; instead, compassion activates the heart to hold you in loving embrace. Right now you can stop feeling guilty. Right now you can stop behaving in ways that don't serve you. Guilt is not a tool to help you remember who you are. If you've done something wrong, just don't do it again. Make amends and move on. Remorse is concluded once you atone for your wrongs. When you use guilt or shame to manage you, you stay in yesterday. You are energetically telling yourself you cannot be trusted. You become your own jailer. Letting go means you've learned what you needed to learn. This is what it means to live with no regrets. When you make amends, you honor your regret. The best medicine for regret is to live better now. By the same token, we cannot hold others in their pain for their wrongdoings. When we forgive, we allow ourselves to heal. If we hold aggression for another, then we are in jail with them. Ask yourself if you want to do time with the person who hurt you.

Compassion does not deny what has happened to you; it does not minimize or frame it as a gift.

This is an opportunity to understand the pain others are carrying and how easy it is to want to give our suffering to someone else. The time has come for you to release yourself from the suffering others have imposed upon you, as well as the suffering you have caused others.

A Conscious No

As you listen to and face your interruptions, you declare: "I am done here." Saying no to the injustice of putting your soul on pause is part of a spiritual journey. "No" is a generous offering to oneself. We don't say no enough. Have you seen a wee one who has learned the power of no and it's all he or she says? Everything is no. And then that child is often talked out of their no, tamed out of their no. Girls in particular lose the generosity of truth that no gives them. As we go along in life we learn to justify why we cannot say no, and then we reinforce the doubt of the power of no by distracting ourselves, circling back into the second-guessing and bargaining behaviors. When you don't say a conscious no, you are saying an *unconscious yes* to something. Saying "No, not in my life," is one of the most elegant acts you can do.

Bow to Your Interruptions

Working with childhood interruptions is not a battle. You don't need to have a face-off. Instead, I'm going to ask you to do something different. Bow to your interruptions. Open the door and let them all come in. Yes, invite them for a visit—all the memories, the interactions, and the pain of being denied your unique nature. There is a conversation you can have, if only to begin the dialogue of acknowledgment that yes this happened to you and yes this is where it ends. It's your life now. My seventh grade math teacher, Mr. Bell, told each child of color that they would never measure up. On the last day of school he handed me my grade, a D+. He leaned down toward me and said, "You should plan on being a domestic worker. That's your best future." He told my Guatemalan friend he should be a landscaper or mechanic. Mr. Bell was a racist who actively discouraged children of color. He attempted to interrupt us. I can forgive Mr. Bell. I can have compassion for his ignorance. I can have compassion for what hate created inside of him. However, I cannot imagine living with hate in me, like a cancer I could not heal. Most interruptions we can handle ourselves when we are willing to face them. It's our unwillingness to face them that has us go down the rabbit hole, never to return. You will know when you need outside help and what you can manage on your own. There is no shame in being interrupted or seeking professional help if you need it.

As you begin to work with your interruptions, you get to decide who and what no longer gets to influence you. Sure, moving the past from being in the lead in your life will take time and effort—the same time and effort you are using to manage those interruptions. Why not use that energy to move through them? You will continuously experience anything you carry inside. You want to pull those weeds instead. The only way to do that is to visit your garden often. Walk around in it and be honest about what you experience. This is your life. This is your world to experience any way you want. You are an adult now. You don't have to go it alone, but only you can do the work. Why not gather others to join you in this journey to be named? Community can hold you more deeply and with the love you need.

Your Holy Nature

In your holy nature you are gifted with the insight to see your internal landscape: the story of what was true about your nature before you were told otherwise. Your internal landscape is a place where you remember that you are gifted as an artist in whatever form that comes to you. Here, the fog that has blurred your vision of who you are is dispersed—replaced by clarity. This is where the story of your calling is waiting to be nurtured into being.

You are creative. Everyone has a creative calling, be it an accountant who is fluent in the language of numbers, or a civil engineer who designs highways and bridges, or a traditionally named artist such as a poet, writer, speaker, or painter. You are an artist. Until you actively receive and nurture your divinity, you are in danger of being separated from it, reduced to managing a life instead of living it. It's astonishing how many people believe that responding to the logistics of life is their path to happiness. They become *responsible* and *appropriate* people who are run by logic. They seek distractions to disrupt the boredom of their life, rather than delving into the mysteries of life and having fun with it.

Be careful as you move along your uninterrupted life to minimize the amount of structure placed there. Structure is made to support you and your beautiful life, not to define it. Your structures should be repurposed throughout your life. You are an ever-evolving being; never allow yourself to become a static one.

The Myth of Safety

Why do we seek the comfort of the known rather than the risk of the unknown? Safety as a place to hide from the risk of life and of love is an illusion. Your marital status, your job, your weight, your age, your money will not make you safe. They make you married and employed, slim or heavy, young or old, financially secure or not, but they don't give you physical, emotional, or spiritual safety. There isn't a guardrail you can put around your experiences to keep them at bay. You will always have some experiences that are easy and others that are hard. You will experience pain and love, and you will have whatever emotion you assign to these experiences. The work is not in keeping yourself safe, but in learning how to navigate the world of your emotions when life happens.

Most of the work done around trying to be emotionally safe is to not feel pain. A life of avoidance is conducted with high levels of stress. Everything has to be navigated; every moment is designed with an eye at being careful, rather than being designed with care. When you operate from a place of caution, you are being triggered by the world of hurt or the perceived hurt of yesterday. You are trying to sidestep the emotion you felt yesterday. You believe you are protecting yourself from pain, when in reality the pain never left you. You are stuck in a slew of rules you've applied to keep you safe, or rather, to keep you stuck. Your triggers are accompanied by outdated responses that you no longer need. Let them fall away. The power emotions have to dictate your experience of life is ready to dissolve, making way for a more confident, brave, self-assured you.

Emotions are information and nothing more.

When you play it safe you have emotional reactions, not emotional responses, and those reactions are not based in current time. The information you are receiving is often inaccurate, old, and irrelevant. It is time to move through that false sense of safety. Trust that you can navigate life as it is. Your holy nature is not negotiable. The wise one, the one who will be named, instinctively hears the misbeliefs about safety and opts for rewriting the corruptions of their story, remembering their holy nature, and honoring their self-knowing.

Recently I walked into a bank to make a deposit. As I stood in line with four others I could see two bank executives checking us out. The unsafe one within me began wondering who was in trouble and what was wrong. When I saw they were staring at me, I wanted to flee for safety. I could feel panic rising.

"Breathe," my wise one said. "Breathe again."

As I approached the teller, the executives came close to me. One of them asked, "What do you do?"

"What?" I replied.

"What do you do?" she asked again. "Because you radiate such love and we want to know what you do."

When we have these alchemical moments, it's an opportunity to reroute ourselves and start heading forward. Otherwise, once we commit ourselves to a scenario, we will continue to find and justify all the reasons why we were right to be afraid.

Your freedom begins now.

Born to Belong, Taught to Conform

Begin to look at the ways in which your "you-ness" was put on pause. Identify those parts of you that were told, "You will not be accepted." We were taught that to belong we must blend. We experience the shame of our unique nature as a motivator to hide, pause, limit, or even delete our original nature. We were born belonging to the world and its inhabitants. But then we were schooled in the classroom of interruptions where we were indoctrinated to fit in and conform.

We substitute our desire for belonging with "fitting in." We search out all the ways we can be validated, hoping that with that stamp of approval we will feel a real connection of belonging. But validation, like being high, dissipates quickly, and the need for it begins again. We are told from grade school to the workplace that if we want to be liked, promoted, and included, we have to amputate our divine nature. We take on facile identities: We become the woman who can do X or the man who is Y. We become the executive so we feel a sense of power, the attorney because it is expected of us, the well-liked coach rather than the fierce artist. We are taught to value catchphrases like "team player," so we alter our behavior, forgetting that true belonging is found in the state of true diversity. In belonging, your diverse tribe doesn't pick and choose the pieces of you that they like and then ask you to keep the other parts quiet. Belonging is the very definition of diversity—in perspectives, in how you live your life, in your unique art and beliefs. Conformity demands an outward appearance of sameness. Conformity is not a part of the natural world. If it were, nothing original could bloom. Nothing creative can be seen in conformity, and yet as humans we can impose this unnatural act on one another.

This is your opportunity to delete the names that are not yours. You will be recalling the next piece of your truth. It truly is a re-calling: a calling yourself back into concordance with your soul. Those places where you manage yourself, where you edit, second-guess, conform, stay silent, or react from yesterday with your protections firmly in place will be shown to the exit.

The Ordinary Journey of Your Unique Nature

If we were all freed from our interruptions and healed from our wounds, being unique wouldn't feel so fragile, so risky. So, I ask you, which story will you listen to: the story that was laid upon you, or the story that was written within your spirit? So much healing is within your hands. When you reclaim the unique aspects of yourself that were put on hold, being unique will feel like putting on a comfortable pair of shoes—with one addition. Joy will be included in the experience. Joy is grounding, not a place of ecstasy. That is the misconception, which is why we think we don't feel joy daily. Joy is enjoying being fully alive—enjoying this moment right here and right now. The word *joy* is one that's used in such a manner that it gives us the illusion that it is only for the enlightened—a holy grail. In reality, joy is simple. It is ordinary. It is meant to be an ordinary experience. Ordinary is not plain, flat, or without flavor. It is simple. It is rich like a delicious piece of chocolate cake. Your everyday joy doesn't need decorations to announce itself. It is there every day, plainly, ordinarily, brilliantly beautiful. This is how nature lives. There is no upsell in nature. It is naturally beautiful, dynamic, and soulful. It's our sight, our listening, that is dulled, not the world.

As you shift your focus away from the stories of interruptions that are replaying themselves in you, joy and the song of the universe will be more accessible. The appeal of the shallow way of life will begin to evaporate. You won't need to be entertained or swept away to be wholly, holy you. You will clear the debris that has fallen atop your joyous self.

The Effort of Being You: How to Tell If You Are on Pause

You're on pause if you have been making yourself larger than life to be heard or seen. You're the one in charge, the one who gives direction, so you influence what happens. You're the one who always has to bring the controversy or the downside to give others a look at what won't work. You pride yourself on being the devil's advocate. You're the one who is stubborn and won't move or do something that is uncomfortable. The stubborn ones are usually quite articulate and sound reasonable, but they are just as stuck as everyone else. Or maybe you are the one who has the latest fashions, the nicest car, the makeup down to a science to gain attention, but you never feel filled up. You are the truth teller who believes in telling the truth at any cost, regardless of the circumstances.

I was mentoring a new coach, and as part of our work together I'd observe her coaching and give her feedback. Feedback can be tricky because you never know what it will trigger in someone. (By the way, triggers are an indication that you have been put on pause.)

"Being bold is necessary, but boldly telling the truth without compassion diminishes the person you're speaking with," I told her.

Her response to me was, "Well, I have to tell the truth at whatever the cost. The truth *is* the truth and that is how I roll."

We know that *how* one says the truth is just as important as the truth itself. We, as humans, need a humane experience. What was the truth of this young coach? *What she had to say was more important than caring for the person's feelings.* She couldn't allow vulnerability to lead because she was working so hard to be heard. Her protection taught her that being heard made her visible, when in fact, the power is always in the presence that listening offers. She was overworking.

When we are overworking aspects of ourselves, we are attempting to prove something to the one who interrupted us, as well as to the wee one inside of us. Proving reinforces the interruptions. It's like pushing up against a fortified door; it will never open that way. In reality there is no door. We cannot prove to ourselves a different reality from the reality we are in. Let's take the doors that lock you in off their hinges.

Overreliance on the Sexual and the Sensual

I honor the sensual and sexual in women, but when I see that all a woman can show is her sexual or sexy self, it tells me that she is fighting against feeling invisible. We know we gain attention when we sexualize ourselves. We live in the land of selfies now, and what we share says everything we hold true about ourselves. Even when that truth is the fear that we will not be seen unless we do what we are told. We are more than what being sexy full time can buy us. Being sexual might get you attention, but it doesn't get you respect or love, and it's not the you who truly wants to be seen. It's what you're settling for in this brief moment, based on your interruption.

Settling is true for all of us who are on pause. Every time you sell your soul with hypersexuality, you reinforce the interruption. The constant attention that goes into the oversell of self is simultaneously denying the whole self. It doesn't help that we are trained in every way possible, from being told we have to hug and kiss people we don't want to as children, to the media selling the sexuality of women as their identity and sole purpose for their relevance.

Denying Your Vulnerability

If you struggle with being vulnerable and letting others hold and see you emotionally and physically, you are interrupting love. Your practice is to notice when you interrupt yourself in this way. Love, like your soon-to-be-discovered name, is nonnegotiable. Yes, you can refuse to accept it, but you cannot negotiate love. Love has its own terms. When you deny vulnerability, you deny wisdom and humility. Denying your vulnerability can play out in the following ways:

- Being busy so you don't have to feel anything.

- Being unable to be quiet or still.

- Using sarcasm, humor, or intelligence as a way to create distance.

- Using sex as a substitute for love.

- Being defensive and unwilling to listen when someone who loves you gives you feedback.

- Not getting the help you need.

- Never asking for help.
- Being overdependent on others to help you live your life.
- Hiding behind logic.
- Pretending to have it all together.
- Using materialism as a booster of self-confidence and worth.

Unlearning these habits and tendencies will feel scary, not because being vulnerable is scary but because going into the unknown isn't something the world values. We are taught to stay with what's comfortable and what we know. We are taught that if we are positive and speak powerful mantras we will be on course. Living the named life, the life of love, is like baking a cake: you can't take out any of the crucial ingredients and still come up with something you'd enjoy eating. Patchworking your spiritual path isn't a path at all. Whatever path you take as the Named One on your journey to your soul's identity, vulnerability is your teacher. Watch it strip away all that is hurt.

An Unwillingness to Be Visible

Are you saying no to your creative ideas or your urgings? Does your inner dialogue sounds like this: *Who would pay for this?* or *Who am I to do this? I have children, I cannot be or do this now. Maybe later, after they are grown.* But if you wait, what are you teaching your children? What you are really saying no to is your life force.

Developing your openness to be fully seen will aid you in releasing interruptions. Being vulnerable is hard work. Letting others in and allowing them to see all your beauty and your warts is challenging. Yet you delve in to soften your heart, to see the world around you in a kinder, more compassionate way. You open yourself to the stream of love, trying to get inside. As you peel the layers off, allowing for a touchable you, you will experience that yes, you *do* belong, you *are* wanted just as you are, and the stories of yesterday begin to be impervious to your present.

Vulnerability makes space for the experiences in life you value, and what you value has space to show you a divine way to experience it. Judgments of self and others lie down, and joy comes to visit for a much longer stay.

Sandi's Story of Being Interrupted

I was 10, in the fifth grade. I was getting high grades and I realized I was pretty good at this school thing if I tried. I loved learning and I loved being good at it.

One afternoon I was talking with my dad, telling him about school and how good my grades were. I said something like, "I am really smart. One of the smartest in my class." I was so full of accomplishment and pride. It felt powerful to know this about myself. As a shy, very introverted, and self-conscious child, this newfound confidence felt wonderful—like I had a place in the world I could depend on. My father listened and then said, "You're being very conceited, aren't you." In that moment I wanted to die. I was ashamed, embarrassed, horrified that I would think such grand things about myself. How could I have been so stupid as to think myself smart, and worse, to seek attention for it? I decided in that moment that it was not okay to be smart. It especially wasn't okay to know myself as smart. That was conceited and one of the absolute worst things to be.

While I loved school and still did well academically, I would dismiss my good grades as "luck," even as I labored so very hard to get them. I would minimize any compliments with listing all the things I did not do right. I would flat-out deny I was smart at all, and absolutely not any better at anything than anyone else! "Don't you see how flawed and imperfect I am?" I would say. "Not special in any way!" I walked a tightrope between having a curious, intelligent nature and not letting myself know it out of fear of being called arrogant, full of myself, better than everyone else.

Over the years this led to hiding how much going to college meant to me, working toward it almost in secret from my family. It meant passing by applying for four-year colleges, because who was I to think a school would want me? I finally graduated in my mid-30s after years of piecing together my education. Along the way something shifted.

Now at 52 I still have moments when my tendency is to hide away, to doubt myself so as not to think myself too grand. But now I say "Thank you" when I am acknowledged or complimented rather than deny or minimize myself. I am thankful and proud of the unique ways of my mind and intelligence. Instead of painfully keeping myself in check so as to not seem egotistical, I unabashedly feed my desire to deepen and expand my knowledge and intelligence. I have claimed freedom to shine my wisdom. Proudly.

Sandi Davis

Sandi was interrupted, just like you. And yet she is strong, brilliant, and fierce, just like you. Sandi is learning to say no to the pause on her self-pride. Interruptions, also known as lies, are visceral. You feel everything you think. When you consciously or unconsciously replay

53

interruptions, you may feel how you felt when you realized what they meant. But perhaps you are not aware of those feelings. Perhaps you numbed out over time. Perhaps, like so many, you heard the interruption that said, "Tell everyone you're fine even when you are not." "Don't let them see you sweat" was a favorite statement of one of my former bosses. It always made me sad when he said that. It made me incredibly sad to believe that we lived in a world in which pretending to have it all together meant you should lead, get the job, be considered worthy, and that anything less meant you were weak.

With your growing awareness, you may be surprised by the many faces of interruption and the ways they show up in your life. The interruptions of the past are not your legacy to live. They were a moment in time, and now is a new moment. These interruptions now call forth great courage, resilience, and the remembrance of who you truly are. You will learn how to note a lie when you hear it and move into your truth. Your time of reconciling the truth with the lie of the past will shorten, because you will become skilled at anything you practice. This also means that living your name and your truth will become easier and more natural the more you do it. Truth doesn't stunt; it doesn't ask you to cut part of your soul out to be included. Remember who you are and bring yourself home to the soul of wholeness.

Be Spacious

Allow yourself to feel what these interruptions do inside your body and grieve in your own way. Grieving is a form of acceptance of what has taken place and a time of moving through. Give yourself time to experience each of these points of disconnection fully. I've coached many a soul who said, "I thought I dealt with that" as though "that" doesn't have its own life span. As you expand out of one interruption, the next one will attempt to come forward. This is normal. When you work in the realm of consciousness, you know that your unconscious will only make visible what you agree your conscious mind can handle. If an interruption should reappear in your life, it will show you a new aspect to accept and release. You will have built your conscious muscle over time and should an old interruption reappear it will feel more like a grain of sand than an entire beach to be combed.

Body-Conscious Listening

When you become acquainted with your interruptions you will begin to notice your body's responses. Every emotion has a response in your body. Feeling angry? Does it start in your throat? Does your face become red? Every emotion has a physical trigger. A gift of flowers makes you feel loved. Being teased reminds you of being ridiculed in grade school. These are accompanied with an emotion. Every emotion also has a behavioral response. You get hurt and shut down. You get angry and pretend you are not, laughing it off, walking away, seeking revenge, exiting the relationship.

The encyclopedia of information in your body is trying to tell you about your interruptions and the behavior and triggers that accompany you wherever you go in life. The responses are exhausting, whether you are aware of this or not. The inquiries below ask for you to bring all your senses forth to reply. Feel into your body to hear the location that responds. It has a story to share with you to help you move forward. Being curious with yourself will support your acceptance and release. Does your stomach feel nauseous? Does your neck tighten? What default behavior wants to interrupt this conversation? Imagine not being hooked, like a fish gasping for air, after being triggered by others unknowingly hitting your pause button.

Day after day you have been governed by responses that you developed to deal with your childhood interruptions. When do you want to be free? I hope the answer is now. No one, no incident, can contain you unless you agree. It's time to be present with yourself, to take a look back to leap forward. It's time to identify the ways in which you were misnamed by a parent, a teacher, a religion, or the prevailing belief of the culture and the society in which you were raised. Deleting what *was* and naming what *is*, you will no longer be asked—by yourself or anyone else—to manage any part of yourself. This is your time to be fully aware of what you are not and to claim who you are.

The Adult Interrupted

The influence of being interrupted doesn't end with childhood. The desire to contain and change others surfs around us as we age. Like thieves in the night, there are societal voices attempting to dictate your surrender of what is precious and beautiful about you. We are told that in order to be professional we must separate who we are at work from who we are everywhere else. We use the words *be professional* as a line of judgment not to be crossed. The workplace tells us, "We want your skills but not your personality, your values, your dreams, or your emotions." As holy beings, we were never created with the ability to separate ourselves into tiny boxes for the comfort of others. We are wholly integrated from the start for the purpose of living our Original Story in hand with our Original Medicine. When we do not operate as such there is abrupt separation anxiety.

Women are continually told the tale of how maintaining perpetual youth and beauty is the only way to guarantee love and admiration. All will continue to be glorious, the story goes, as long as they don't appear to have really aged. The monster in the woods is an old woman whose flesh has folded and creased—unsightly to look at, she is banished from the world. The all-pervasive narrative of what a woman should weigh and look like is a poison to the soul, and many of us have drunk this poison from early on in life.

We pause our intuition, our own listening, our own path for the undeveloped articles and blogs promising relief and redemption if we do "five simple things" to keep ourselves relevant. Other articles tell us that women become invisible after a certain age and so we must do this and that before it's too late. Women of all ages continue to be told that their value is sexual. Yes, the world is changing, but these messages still exist.

Men are interrupted when they are taught that the measure of their worth is intrinsically tied to how much money they have, their job title, their athletic ability, their sexual prowess, and their intelligence. Men who become unemployed or underemployed sink into a deep depression because all they have strived for seems unattainable. Men are told directly and indirectly, from cartoons to commercials, that feeling and expressing emotions is off-limits. What kind of men are we growing when we impede them to such a degree? It is common for both women and men to be so hungry to feel something—anything—that they reach for the closest acceptable feeling, which is sexual power, or at its lowest consciousness, lust, and opt for sexual encounters with no real love.

The named path encourages you to be a troublemaker, a seeker of your truth, a yearner of wisdom and real love. Don't buy into the soul-bending beliefs of your culture, society, church, friends, or family. Trust your internal wisdom and disobey the rules someone else has made up for you. You are encouraged to speak up, to share your truth, to pursue your form of art, and to do it unencumbered. Your work on this path is in learning to say no in balance with the yes of your soul. Your work is to stay in communion with your beauty, your truth, and your self-love. Go out into the world recalling, reclaiming, knowing you are made whole. This is what courage, self-worth, and daring to be you look like. You will need them. You are braver than you know. Call yourself forward.

A Blessing

You are about to cross a threshold from the story of interruption into the land of self-knowing, forgiveness, letting go, and standing in your authority. Forgiveness is a medicine we all carry. It drops the weight of those heavy stones that keep us at the bottom of life gasping for air. Forgiveness stops the debilitating war within that you may not even be aware of. You are a blessing and you are blessed. In these moments you take yourself off pause and you continue on your path to wholeness, beauty, peace, and love. This blessing is to swaddle you as you enter the next realm of certain humble knowing. If it's helpful, you can record this in your own words and play it back to allow the verbal vibration of the truth to beat its rhythm right into your soul.

May you be released in total from erroneous interruptions and influences.

May you be restored completely into your own knowing.

May you accept your generative nature and feel yourself coming back into full congruency with Mother Earth, Father Sky, all that lives in the wild, and the wild inside you.

May you receive the love pouring into you from the ancients.

May you love so deeply it brings tears of joy.

May you be so strong and brave that you show every wart and bump to all, knowing we will caress and kiss them in adoration.

May you embrace the peace within as you live your Original Story and honor your Original Medicine.

May you feel the belonging to all that ever was and shall be.

The Practice: Identifying How You Were Paused

Time: 90 minutes
Materials: journal and pen

You felt pain when you were being interrupted, and you will feel pain as you expand out of these interruptions. Pain is part of the process, but how much pain you feel and how often you associate with it is in your hands. And what you do with the pain is always in your hands. Naming what has been put on pause is challenging work. You are challenging all the negative voices, including your own. Your negative voice wants employment. It believes it is serving you well. But love never makes you second-guess. It never keeps you stuck or on pause. Discern what is healthy on your own terms.

As you move through your interruptions, you may feel outrage, sadness, and nervousness. But ultimately, with time, you will feel freedom. Give yourself ample space to do this work. Emotions are simply information; they are not a dictate you need to follow through on.

Grab your journal, breathe, and with your willing heart take an earnest turn at naming what aspects of you have been put on pause by answering these prompts below:

- Identify each person who interrupted you.

- What were you told that interrupted your divine nature?

- What was said to you and how was it said?

- What behavior did you employ that keeps you interrupted?

- Was it a look or an act?

- What splendor got shut down in you?

- What would you do if you had the skills back then that you do now?

- What was so rich in you that you want to recall back now?

Breathe.

You can believe this: when someone interrupts you, it tells you how interrupted they are. It tells you about their consciousness. Going forward, you never have to take on what another person gives you, especially if it doesn't fit. You never have to feel angry, bad, or frustrated with another. Know that their attempt is their shit. Know

now who you are and who you are not. An interruption is an attempt from another to misname you.

The Practice: Rearranging the Past to Accommodate the Truth of Your Present

Time: 20–30 minutes
Materials: recorder, journal, and pen

Do this exercise when you feel the most positive in your day.

Record the following instructions on your smartphone. This will allow you to replay them and to be present with the practice. Begin with recording your "I am" statement and then record the time line practice that follows.

Start by creating a soul-truth statement that calls your self back into you. For example: *I always have been brilliant. I use my brilliance to change my life.* Or make a powerful "I am" statement. Here is Sandi's "I am" statement:

> *The invitation for me has arrived and I accept*
> *I am always invited to the table.*
> *I am not bound to the falsity of my past.*
> *The sensual calls me to speak of it with all the beauty*
> *I am.*

Make it true and keep it simple. Write it down in your journal. Once you have your statement of absolute truth and soul-honoring, keep it in your mind and heart.

The Practice: Time Line

Now close your eyes. See in your mind's eye a time line that starts at the point of your first interruption and extends to today. A time line is a straight line that charts a year and days. See the past—as far back as your first interruption—on the left or closer to you. See the present moment at the end, to the right or further away from you. Once you see that time line in your mind, see yourself walking up to the time line. Hop up on the time line and walk back to the time of your first interruption. While standing on the time line, see in your mind the person or situation that interrupted you. (If you can't recall the person or situation, face the past near the year of your earliest memory of the interruption.) Now say what you need to say to recall your self back into being the joyous, divine-natured being that you are. For example, Sandi's father called her conceited. On her time line, January 1970 is when she faces that interruption; she feels it and now brings her truth forward to meet the interruption. Looking at the interruption, she says: "I am not conceited. I am proud. You are confused. You have no power to continue to interrupt me. I am brilliant and use my brilliance to change my life and the lives of my clients."

Speak to each person, each interruption, one by one. Move forward on the time line. When you are finished, face the past interruptions and delete them by telling them you forgive them. If you cannot say it, continue to do this exercise until you can. Forgiving them doesn't release them from their responsibility; it releases their hold on you. Forgiveness is you giving yourself freedom. Until you forgive, you will hold on to the memory that jails you. Your forgiveness is the bringer of peace in your own heart.

Once you've had that conversation, walk forward to the present. Note today's date in your mind. See the paper that you wrote your soul truth on in your mind. In your mind hold that soul truth right above today and let it float down into the time line. The time line is an active, vibrating energy that will absorb your truth. Now turn toward the past one last time, watching your time line rearranging the past to accommodate your soul's truth. Turn toward the present and look toward the future, watching your time line arranging itself to include this new truth. Accept that life has arranged itself to accommodate this new truth. Good. Now, jump off the time line and come back into now, knowing it's done. Say to yourself aloud: "My soul's truth is with me forevermore. I am free. I am whole. I am love. I am loved." Come back into the here and now. Open your eyes. Stretch your body and take a well-deserved break.

The Practice: Caring for the Inner Child

Time: 20 minutes
Materials: recorder

If you have just completed the previous practices, wait at least an hour before you do this one.

Turn off everything digital, except for your recording device. If you are using a smartphone as a recorder, set it to "airplane mode" and silence the ringer. Similar to the practice above, you will create a movie in your mind to reconfigure your past. In this practice, your adult and child selves come together to create a new reality. Read through the visualization first and then record the visualization ahead of time.

Now breathe four full breaths to help quiet your mind. Practice being still and quiet. Notice how soothing it is to your mind to be still and quiet. Breathe. Take your time breathing in and breathing out. Let your eyes close. Feel what it's like to take a breath. Become conscious of your breath. Take four more full belly breaths and exhale each slowly. Relax your shoulders and back. Relax your jaw. Move down your body, intentionally relaxing. Breathe.

At the count of three you are going to create a movie in your mind. Some people call this using your third eye because it's the space between your eyes. You are going to use that space between your eyes to do some visioning.

Bring up a movie screen in your mind.

See it there. Large enough to hold your vision of yourself.

You are seated in a beautiful theater. It's just you there for this private screening.

You're safe and comfortable.

Now bring to the screen you at the age of your first interruption. Leave the interruption, just bring up the image of you at the age when it took place.

Where are you? Wherever you are, know you are in a safe and loving place.

Acknowledge within your heart how beautiful, creative, and loving you are. See yourself on the movie screen. See your innocence. See how beautiful you are. As you see and feel this you, take your index finger and tap your third eye twice. You are putting that image right inside your mind to keep.

Again, see this you, feel this you, and tap, tap.

Once more, see this you, feel this you, and tap, tap.

Good. Breathe.

Now bring your current self into the movie. Move your current self toward your younger self and say hello. Introduce yourself. You can say, "I'm you, just older."

Take two minutes and in your own words tell your younger self how you will take care of him/her from now on. Tell your younger self that life is safe, the world is safe to be exactly as you were, that there are no interruptions keeping you from being self-expressed, self-loved, and self-honoring.

Good.

Should your mind wander, breathe and come back to your movie.

Now bring to the screen a time in your life when you were interrupted. Play the entire interruption out. Breathe. Once you've played it out fully, call forward the person or situation in still form and pause your movie.

In your mind's eye, enter into the movie again as you are now. In your own way, say what you need to say to conclude this event. You can say, "I forgive you," "I release you," or anything else that makes it complete for you. You can tell the person or situation how he/she/it interrupted you and the impact that had on your life.

When you are done, say, "I release you."

Put your index finger on your heart and tap twice.

Breathe.

Watch the person or situation easily fade like a cloud.

Put your index finger on your third eye and tap twice.

Then again, put your index finger on your heart and tap twice.

Turn your back on the faded person or situation and face your future.

Good.

Notice in your hand is a sheet of paper that has written on it "I'm whole, I'm loved, and free to be me completely me." Standing at today, watch your time line open up right at today and before tomorrow. When you're ready, release the sheet of paper and watch as it lands on today's date.

Breathe.

Now look toward tomorrow and the beyond. Notice that your time line is rearranging itself to accommodate your truth, right now.

Breathe. Tap twice on your heart.

Jump off your time line, landing easily and safely into right now, where you are sitting and watching your movie, knowing that you have already shifted. Tap twice on your heart.

Breathe.

Before you come back into your body and open your eyes, tell yourself you will always be loving to yourself in thought, word, and deed.

Take your index finger and touch your heart. Tap twice.

Breathe.

Touch your heart and tap, tap.

Breathe.

Touch your heart and tap, tap.

Touch your third eye and tap, tap.

On the count of one, you will come back into your body in this present moment.

Two, you are loved now and forever. Stretch your arms over your head.

Three, you are ready to move forward. Stretch your legs, coming back into your body, knowing everything you did in your mind's movie is real and will occur as you directed.

If the past calls you, don't answer. When you hear that knock at the door, touch your third eye and tap, tap. Touch your heart and tap, tap. Seal it with a warm and earnest smile. Breathe and keep moving forward.

Be You

Every hour in every day do what has always come naturally: do "you." Remember who you are and honor that. Stand tall for your profundity. All that really matters is you loving your creative nature and living. Life seems to fall into place when you dance your dance. The tough parts of life are still there. The sad parts of life are still there. But you being and doing you means there is less to navigate around and through. These interruptions are not unique to you. We all get some version of them. Don't allow your miracle to be embroiled in the mundane nature of someone else's pain. As you stand in your true self, the amount of pain you pass on will also diminish. In the circle of belonging, we begin to take an active role in being responsible for our impact, knowing that it often begins with noticing how we, ourselves, have been impacted.

Chapter 4

YOUR ORIGINAL STORY AND ORIGINAL MEDICINE

You are born with an Original Story embroidered into your very soul. It is the story of your unique offering to the world and it fires the engine for how you present your art in the world. (Remember, I use *art* as an all-encompassing term for everything that is creative in your life.) Your Original Story is the prayer of who you are. Some might call this your life purpose. I think of it as what you cannot help but be in the world. Your Original Story is how you walk in this beautiful world. It isn't how you've learned to negotiate your walk as the shielded or interrupted one. It is your organic nature of fire, elegance, and poetry. It is what is unique about how you see and interact with the world. With each step you share your story with us.

Your Original Story begins as a thread. Each day, every decision, every new learning and lesson reveal an ancient and divine poem written in harmony with your soul's desire. With the space you made by decluttering the interruptions and your continued presence through sacred listening, more of your story can drop down for you to acknowledge. Your story is also revealed in relationship to others. You interact and someone inspires a new conversation your mind has not held before. Another person irritates you, unveiling a new purpose for you to attend and bend into. The evolution of you through your Original Story is certain. You will know you are walking in your story when the second-guessing of the ego begins or when another person makes a judgmental inquiry about why you are the way you are and it doesn't change your swagger. You have subscribed to your truth and nothing catches you off balance anymore.

Each of us has an Original Story that is unfolding in each moment, though many people do not hear their story, do not cultivate their wisdom, and do not know they have a story at all. This is not the story of life events, past pain or gain; it's the story of your soul. It's speaking to you at this very moment.

Being named has not been the easiest path. You arrived here via a stripping down, a path of deconstruction—a destruction of all the impasses that have kept you from your knowing. And now you are here. You've laid down and let go of the obstacles that obstructed your view of your temple within. Your Original Story puts you on the path to acknowledging yourself. It's time to learn how to walk in your own authority. Your presence commands a level of respect and pride for you to own. The one who shares his or her Original Story walks in grace, lovingly holding it to share in all ways of being and doing. Your Original Story is based in love and includes all your experiences. Love strips us of what we think we know, of what we think we are, and opens our pores, filling them with truth.

Your Tribal Nature

Your Original Story is woven into the tapestry of all that has ever lived. We belong to one another, but this is not the story most of us are told. We are tribal in nature, though for many of us that desire has been interrupted. Tribes approach relationships as necessary and interdependent. They cannot live without one another, for each person brings their piece of the tapestry, their Original Story, and this keeps the teepee standing and the fires burning. You are indigenous to the world. Indigenous means to be a native to where you are. As an indigenous person, you belong to this landscape, adding in your beauty and thriving in the beauty of others. This is your tribe and you belong here. This interdependence keeps your heart loved, your body nourished, your mind brave, and your spirit generative and evolving. Communities elicit the exact nature of your story to add to the collective well-being of others. There is no "Go figure it out" or "Pull yourself up by your bootstraps" kind of thinking. It is the elders showing the young ones the way and allowing them to try, fail, and learn as they are held in the community. If we remembered that we belonged to one other, that we were one tribe, one community, we could not be bought or sold as easily as we are in the many ways that currently occur.

In interdependence we count on one another in order to survive. We need your skill, your talents, your "being-ness" in order to know our own. Community presents a state of holy communion—an organic stance of needing the beauty in one another in order to be connected to the universe. Instead, we have settled for clubs. Clubs are where we gather for the purpose of sharing a common interest. Clubs have their purpose, but belonging in this context is only true when we are the same in a club sharing

71

the same ideals. Diversity is the organic nature of community, and in our diverse nature we are rooted in our Original Story, stronger, happier, and healthier for it. To live in this dynamic, ever-evolving nature, you have to agree to live your Original Story. Without your gift of a story well walked, there is no diversity, no range, no evolution.

In a world without true belonging (the kind that comes from a tribal community), our threading comes loose. There is no firm, consistent support holding us together. Anything can slip in—comparison, envy, self-doubt, the undoing of one's self. We are so hungry for the nurturing sap of life that we gather in clubs and convince ourselves it's a community. But we are not communing; we are assembling. Naming is the path of belonging, and you belong here.

Like the petroglyphs of the ancients' stories on the cave walls, your story is etched within. As your story unfolds in your lifetime, you will be called to a remodel of your personality. The personality is like a chariot. Your soul is the driver. Our world often confuses these roles. Living as the Named One you will become adept at remodeling your personality to execute the directives of your soul. In a tribal community, you are an individual who is unique without being separate from the whole. Imagine no longer needing validation in the vast way most humans need it again and again, never believing it, always trying to fill a bottomless pit.

Your Original Medicine

Learning to intentionally walk with your Original Story will reveal your Original Medicine. Your Original Story may or may not be your purpose in life, but it will lead you to uncover it. As you walk into your Original

Story you become introduced to your Original Medicine. You cannot have one without the other. They are wedded to each other and to you. Your medicine is the manner in which you bring your story to life. It's how you are in your world. Your particular mannerisms, your voice, your specific humanity are part of your medicine. Any time you water down how you do you in the world, you dilute your medicinal properties, rendering them ineffective. Over time not being who you are will become toxic to yourself and all others. Your Original Story may reveal that you are a healer. Your Original Medicine will show you how you heal. It will display how your healing is unique. This is why it's so important not to allow comparison to inform you. Comparison is the thief of joy. It is also why you should never seek to be "normal." There is no such thing as normal. It's a lie and a myth created in an attempt to coerce you into abandoning your medicine and story so you will comply with the demands of the ego and the larger culture. You are not normal. Count this as a blessing. You are gifted. Giftedness is the first definition of diversity. We only have to walk out our door to view how beautifully nature honors diversity and to understand how destructive sameness would be.

Your particular medicine heals others by proxy. You being who you are quietly speaks to others' consciousness to discover what is available for themselves. We easily identify our pains and interruptions as something within us. If only we could have the same ease in identifying our unique brilliance and divine Original Medicine. We are so quick to note our shortcomings but we have to be pushed and pulled into the truth of ourselves as divine blessings. Your medicine is what restores and heals you in cases such as being interrupted. In the Native tradition our medicine comes to us in various ways and it is always associated with the natural world. Our relatives may name our medicine for us, for their wisdom sees it when we are wee ones. Others discover their own medicine in the dream world or through ceremony. And like you, we either deny or accept it. It can feel too big to own. We can question ourselves. It's a useless conversation because eventually the forces of love give us all opportunities to visit with and own our medicine.

You are fire and you bring your fire in by creating your Original Medicine in whatever you do, be it a service, a product, a mannerism. Maybe you are a speaker who challenges us to rise in the face of confrontation. Perhaps you are the bringer of peace. Your Original Story may be one of inclusion and presence, and your medicine of peace allows that to come forward from others easily. People are willing to cooperate when you are there. This is how your medicine impacts the outer world, but your Original Medicine is primarily for you.

I first learned about what I call Original Medicine from watching folks on the reservation becoming fully present. They were themselves: some wild, some quiet, some medicine women, others weavers and beaders. Truth be told, I don't know what their specific vocations were. Their wisdom served the younger ones by how they stood in their authority, how they spoke without wavering, how they could be self-owning yet humble. It was clear that they were comfortable standing in their medicine.

Sometimes the ceremonies we do are hard on our bodies and our psyches. Sometimes we do the ceremonies together. Others are done solo. I'm always entranced by what medicine people bring into the ceremonies we do together. Michele Justice is that one person who always brings compassion and soothing as we start to bicker on day three of a four-day ceremony because we are tired, hungry, and thirsty. Andrea brings fire and calls us forth to go yet one more day. Pablo personally brings the medicine of the songs forward. Another tells stories and jokes that get us in full belly laughter, allowing us to bring in the healing nature it offers. For many years Phil Sitting Bull would bring his Heyoka medicine. A Heyoka, in the Lakota tradition, is the contrarian, the one who does everything opposite or backward. If there was a ceremony with no food or water, Phil would show up with watermelon, eating it in front of us. In one ceremony he poured water over our heads, tempting us to taste it. His medicine was part jester. In my estimation, his medicine was to help us focus on our prayers. Would we focus on our hunger and the watermelon, or our prayers? Crazy Bull also was a healer: more than once, he called in thunder and rain when the forecasted temperature was over 100 degrees. In a group, a medicine can get conjured up among all of us. We create this broth that keeps us bonded to one another. Together there is an invisible but felt commitment to move through what is in front of us, for ourselves and for one another. And while each person brings something, their unique medicine is so much fuller than what we can see from the outside. They can pull out of their soul medicine what is needed from them

The grandmothers and grandfathers gather us up to share their stories, bringing their medicine of wisdom, which they pour into us, asking us to remember what is really important, what is truly relevant. Often the elders will take hours to share their stories, imparting their medicine of knowledge, wisdom, evolution, patience, and learning of the traditional ways of connections with the earth. As we sit in a circle to hear their ancient wisdom, what medicine that is ours to take gets in. We each hear what we need and leave with that medicine folded into us. This is one way our continued evolution is cultivated.

Your Original Story works like the elders speaking to you. It is seeding you with your Original Medicine. Everyone's story begins with knowing that we are of God. Living and loving in alignment with our story and our medicine is how we bring heaven to earth.

Every medicine bundle is created for you to experience your godlike self. You will never look to another to compare yourself or judge them. You will move from desiring freedom to attaining it. You will shine so brilliantly, filled with so much joy as you use your divine spark to light you up, and in doing so you will add that much more light to the world. In living your story and your medicine, you belong. You belong to yourself wholly as the blessing of your story and medicine. This is where true belonging lives. When you stand in your authority and own that you belong here as a gifted soul, you belong to the world and the universe, and you know it.

Walking between Worlds

Your story and medicine are inextricably bonded to each other. Your story and your medicine give you the agility to navigate between the realm of being a human and the realm of being a spirit. You, as the Named One, are spirit. By following your internal nature, you are able to walk on your journey of being spiritual. You are both spirit and human, and you will learn how to live from them both.

My Dinè (Navajo) brother Shorty Baldwin added his artistry to my new pipe, which my elder Pablo and I made. Pablo and I had done the rough cut, but it wasn't a pipe ready to be carried. Honestly, it was an eyesore. Pablo asked Shorty to put his medicine (his art) on my pipe before it was to be blessed. When I arrived at Shorty's home on the

Tsa Ya Toh Reservation, he sat me down to tell me how he came to design my pipe. He told me how he dreamed of the pipe and was told by my ancestors how it should look. As part of his design he etched in two parallel lines of tiny circles with a small space between them. Shorty told me, "The space between the line represents the space between the spirit and the human world. The lines represent the two worlds you walk in and the circles are the Star Nation."

What Shorty was saying to me—and to you—is that we can walk between these two realms. We can bring the spiritual realm into the earthly realm if we believe it and behave accordingly. Every day, wake up ready to listen to your spirit. Every day, let your spirit show you more of how to be with your Original Medicine. Every day, bring heaven to earth.

When I used to arrive home from ceremonies, my body would be in shock upon returning to the earthly realm. I'd call Pablo in tears saying how I didn't want to come back and he'd direct me to go speak to the Star Nation, to have a talk with them and listen to their directives. Their directives were always the same. As my friend Michele would say, "Bring the prayer into everyday life and they, the earth and the spirit, become one and the same."

The Power of Naming What Is Sacred

Tsa Ya Toh (pronounced say ya toe), the name of the reservation where Shorty and Uncle Everett live and where we hold our ceremonies, means Water Under the Rock. Every indigenous culture names what they hold sacred. We name mountains, land, each other, bodies of water, and our animals to honor them. When we call their name we remember their sacred nature and treat them as such. Naming calls us into a state of holy communion. It's important for you to hear that again. What you name you are to live with in holy communion. We live the prayer Mitakuye Oyasin, "We Are All Related." You cannot be named without the recognition that all others are your larger family. You have a connection and a responsibility to love and care for all humanity, the animals, and the earth. When you bring heaven to earth you will experience the freedom that responsibility gives you. It's not the burden we associate with responsibility. The pure form of love cares without sacrifice or the experience of burden or duty. Naming is a ceremony that recognizes you and your relationship with the whole. You are part of that whole and as such you must learn to regard yourself as sacred. Be mindful of how you talk to yourself and about yourself. Be mindful of how you care for yourself. I've seen people treat their pipe better than they treat themselves.

Your Generous Nature

As you walk your walk, you share your medicine by being fully and wholly you every day. This is the most generous act you can give to the world—to be you. Give your spirit to each of us by honoring your soul. When you are consciously aware of your medicine, you use it to heal yourself. In this way you bind your soul, your humanity, to all that ever lived and will live. Being bonded to every living thing means that which does not give life will naturally fall away.

Medicine in the natural world generously gives itself and its medicinal properties to all. Soil lends its medicine to the worms and the trees. Trees lend their properties to the winged ones, the birds, and the creepy crawlers. Each living creature—plant or animal—gives its medicinal properties to all its relatives, which include us humans. They remember that we are related. We are the only species that has the luxury to forget that. The tree in a forest will tell you stories if you listen. The Star Nation will give you guidance if you ask. Bodies of water will soothe you, allowing you to float, to experience the feeling of being buoyed up in them, to feed from them, and to heal. When we bring the sacred water into the *innipi*, the sweat lodge, we say this prayer of recognition of the holy properties of water: mni wichòni, mni wakan (water of life, water is sacred). Nature is unmoved by judgment or usury by others. It continues to be what it is and live in alignment. It is why you feel so joyous in the company of nature. You are receiving the bounty of nature's beauty, truth, and love. Your beauty, truth, and love medicine unfolds this way. You deserve to know yourself this way. When you are in concert with your nature and the natural world, nothing is taken for granted.

What Is Your Original Story?

Together, your Original Story and your Original Medicine are the compass within. You will always know where you are as you live into your story. You will always be guided into the story that is ever unfolding. Your story and medicine are initially yours alone. Others will inherit the benevolence and benefits of your story by way of you being you. Now you can understand how being you is truly an act of generosity. I have heard people say they want to save the world. Save yourself and all your work will be done. Live your Original Story, drink your own Original Medicine, and all will be healed. It is truly that simple.

What does that mean for the one who shall be named to find his or her story? It means to stand in and state your truth. You may not have it all woven together but you have aspects. You have the threads. Anything less than your Original Story and your Original Medicine is a distraction from your truth. Keep yourself centered in truth. Your truth harbors benevolence for you and all those whose path you cross. It is a giving of goodwill to others to stand in your soul-knowing truth.

A former client, Arielle, pretends she doesn't fully understand her story of "she who cares for the forgotten." A teacher, she is equally smart and clever in the way she cares for special-needs children. With a limited budget she has brought innovative and needed services to attend to these children. Her predecessors only saw the limitations of the budget. They didn't have Arielle's dangerous nature that had her take a stand for a population when others would not. Her story gave her initiative to be responsible for their needs. Her medicine told her how and gave her insights and answers that others could not conceive. Every day she rewrites the way these wee ones are supported. But in her personal life Arielle ignores her immense spiritual power only to use it when it is self-serving in a material way. She refuses to change her thought-action-speaking paradigm because it would mean facing her demons, the places where she was interrupted. When life isn't magically arranged to accommodate her, the child victim arises and powerlessness owns her and keeps her interrupted. I see her story; I'm sure many do. Her story is elegantly powerful. Her story and medicine have much more to give her. Many of us use our story and medicine for others even though they are within us initially for our use. When we use our powers solely for others we do so in tandem with the intellect. The originator of who we are is the soul. The soul is the source who teaches us how to evolve and grow into our medicine and our story. Our intellect will find creative ways to use them, to even manipulate them, but it cannot evolve them.

Vickie's Original Story and Medicine

My chosen sister Vickie speaks on the power of her Original Story and Medicine. A young Dinè woman who walks well in both worlds of spirit and flesh, she shares with you what she knows of herself:

Creating connections. Life's journey is not meant to be experienced alone. With each breath, step, action taken, connection is happening all around us.

As I reflect upon my life's journey, I recognize my medicine is of bringing people together. It is a privilege for me to make connections between people with different backgrounds, experiences, knowledge, and reasons for coming together.

When we are present—mindfully present—we can connect with intention and on a deeper level. This connection can lead us to new insights, experiences, wisdom, and knowing that we are a part of something bigger.

Our work is to move past fear, and toward connections. Whether we fear rejection, not belonging, or unmet expectations, through our journey we realize that we are all the same; we are one, all connected. As our ability to make meaningful connections strengthens, we realize what belongs to us . . . each other.

Vickie Kitseallyboy Oldman
Navajo name: T'aa'a tso shi'holo "All that belongs to me"

I had no understanding of my Original Story until well into my 30s when my first Native American elder, George Martin, brought me onto the Red Road. He held the traditions as his elders did, never shortening them or accommodating the impatience of a woman who didn't know she didn't know. As I stepped onto this path I rose each Saturday at 3:30 in the morning to drive two hours to set up the sweat lodge for the ceremony. George made it clear to me from day one: I was not there to be a surveyor of the ceremonial world; I was going to be all-in every Saturday for four years, no excuses. If he was going to show up to teach me, I would be there, too. George held to the traditional ways. He, like all my Native elders, had three ways of imparting learning and wisdom:

1. Do it, be corrected, and learn it.

2. Observe and learn without questioning.

3. Watch and listen to your elders.

George taught in silence. He was strict in his direction, tough in his demeanor. I could feel his Original Story was in teaching the young ones the traditions of his elders without compromise. On my first vision quest, I was visited by an eagle who spoke to me. I left George on the advice of this eagle. George didn't know how to love yet. I was told that I had plenty of rough angry edges within me and that being taught more of this would stunt me, however benevolent his intention. Unadulterated love would have to be part of the teachings I needed to learn, and for now that could not come from George. Saying no to George was not easy for me, nor him. We would not speak again for almost a decade.

While under his tutelage, I learned to hold fast to the legacies, to respect the ways of the old ones, and to not be afraid to say, "No, not this for me." Perhaps we came together for him to teach me to give myself and my Original Story more attention, rather than simply following rules and being obedient. Perhaps our stories were meant to intersect to support the next chapter in each of our lives.

George's story started to unfold almost 10 years later when he was well into his 70s. There is so much beauty, tenderness, and love in him, perhaps for the first time in his life. Maybe it was the last chapter in a series of stories for him. Whatever it was, he had become a wise elder, the one we listen to. He began sharing his wisdom with compassion and love, something I didn't have access to years before. Once at the Sundance ceremony he inquired on how I was doing. I couldn't be tough for him. I replied, "Doing the best I can, George." He smiled at me and said, "That's all we can ask." A compassionate response. In that moment, I was reunited with him. The chapter, from years ago, had an elegant conclusion.

Your journey is so full of wondrous encounters it promises never to end. The joy in this is that we are never done. The chapters keep writing themselves into us. Isn't that glorious? Transformation is continuous. The story keeps unfolding, as long as we are willing to carry it forward. Your medicine bundle will continue to give you new life and new experiences. As you live fully into your name, your name will evolve you and your perspectives.

Each one who will be named will take this deeply personal journey to transform. The journey is ragged with sharp edges that cut away at your dead skin, releasing you from the structures that hold you back from what awaits you. The journey is also glorious and freeing and sometimes dangerous. Danger is not peril. It is who you become when you risk being the fierce courageous one— the one who faces forward. The one who learns from the past but does not live from it. You have no control over what you will find or what you will be asked. You don't know who you are becoming and how the world will receive you. This interior journey is the way of the soulful one. It is dark. It is dangerous. And it is beautiful. Listening for and scribing your Original Story takes you into the dark caverns of tomorrow, taking you "off-road" to have another look at what got buried underground so you can move past those childhood interruptions.

True, it is often ugly before the light shines your path out of the darkness. This time you go willingly, seeing your life within the safety of adulthood. As you walk through your old story to uncover your Original Story, you will encounter the path of beauty that is segued right out of all that was interrupted. You will recall your organic nature. You will celebrate with a deserved righteousness what you already knew was true. You will remember who you are. Once you have that awareness, who you are will be prompted throughout your life to evolve, to add chapter upon chapter of a well-written you. And this is beautiful.

Heather's Original Story

Heather heard her Original Story when she was a child. I think we each hear ours as youngsters but we don't understand what it is or we get interrupted, told not to pay attention to it, and then we forget about it. But you will be escorted back to yourself in a myriad of ways. Here is how Heather was guided back.

When I was in Grade 8, I declared the life I wanted and set out to create it. I started university, and after just one semester, I knew deep down in my soul the path I was on wasn't the one for me. I was uninspired at the thought of going back after the Christmas break, but I had publicly declared a specific path and there was no going back. I see now I created a path built on the expectations of others. It literally took a random serious physical injury to make it okay to drop out. What I needed on a soul level was not reason enough.

By all external measures, I was living the dream: Fortune 500 vice president by the age of 40, a big house in the 'burbs, travel, a growing retirement account. Different circumstances but [sigh] I recognized this place. It literally took a job elimination to have a legitimate excuse to make a career change. What I needed on a soul level was to live more of my Original Story.

Unless I learned the lesson from a specific experience, I was destined to repeat it until I became the lesson. After 15 years as an entrepreneur, I am in the process of finally learning my critical lessons. I no longer rely on external factors to justify the changes I make in my life. I am learning the whisperings of my soul are reason enough. I am learning when I listen to the judgments of others versus my soul, the decisions I make are not in my best interest. Ironically, this wisdom was always available to me. The difference now? I stop to check in with my soul and allow the whisperings to guide me.

Heather knows her Original Story is to help executives remember their humanity. It's easy to forget to take care of oneself when you are taking care of big budgets and big staffs. She knows that making a company grow means the people who lead have to grow and be better people.

The Practice: Writing Your Original Story and Discovering Your Original Medicine

You are about to transcribe your Original Story and Original Medicine. Notice, I said *transcribe*, not write. You are transcribing what has already been written. Create the space to receive. Start by accepting that you are brave enough to take pen to paper to honor your truth.

You can see from Vickie's example that an Original Story and Medicine need not be long-winded. The longer you write, the more often the ego can slip in, attempting forgery. The more you write, the easier it is for fear to write for you. Transcribe. Trust the voice of your Original Story. Trust that interruptions are no longer present and thus will not send a representative to speak here. Below are a few prompts to support you hearing the voice. Use them if they are helpful. Trust that you know this. This is not a mystery to you. Do your best not to hedge or stop the process with thinking, editing, or rearranging. Just write. Other distractions will beg for your attention. Breathe through them. Trust what you receive.

I have one *don't*: I love collage boards but I ask that you not collage your story until the words are out. There is a way we can hide behind the pictures, never allowing the words to push between our lips. So transcribe, and then read what you've written—not to perfect it, but to hear yourself speak your truth. If visuals are your thing, then after you've written and read your story aloud, put images to it to see your story and speak it aloud once more.

Time: 30 minutes
Materials: journal and pen

Before you begin, I want to put in you:

We call in all the angels that represent unbinding truth to support the clear hearing from this soul who will be named.
You are here to be heard.
May you be present to your story and your medicine from now and forever.
May you now hear your divine mandate.
May you live fully in the ever-blossoming of this story and medicine.
May you be humbled by your own beauty.
May your newfound wisdom rise through your heart to lead you from here.
And may it be so.

Original Story Prompts

- What in your soul calls you into belonging? (Example: I'm called to see between the lines in which we attempt to live. I am destruction. I support the eradication of those limits. I am a seer and I call forth your remembrance of your self.)

- What will you experience when you answer the soul's call to belong?

- What have you always known about who you are?

- What is your air?

- What can you not help but be in the world?

- What have you been told by others that they love and don't love about you?

Original Medicine Prompts

- When you live what you know of you, how does it look? What does it do?

- What does it achieve and what is the impact of your knowing?

- What freedom does your medicine grant you?

- What healing will your medicine give you?

- What do you have to shed to step into this place of belonging?

- What will we experience of you as you belong to this you?

- How do you release any fear of being what you are called into?

- What medicine have you always had that is ready to be named and that you will share as you live into this belonging?

- How do you live in your Original Medicine in a world that wants to negotiate everything that is soul deep?

- How did you come to know your medicine?

After your transcribing is complete, use this if it is helpful.

- What have you left out?

- What words are being used that are too small?

- What will you accept as truth and how would anyone know this?

- What help do you need now that you know your story?

- Who do you see in you now?

Keep what you have transcribed close to you. Read it. Speak it 10 times per day for a week. Speak slowly to give it the space to anchor within you. Each time you speak it, you are creating a new legacy within your body that you will be self-fulfilling. Give this truth time to take root before you share it. When we give away our knowing before we know it well, it has a way of being corrupted and vanishing. No one else can hold your truth for you. You need to walk in this before it's ready to be shared. As you live into your story and medicine, you can share what you know with one or two people who have stories big enough to hold yours. You're not asking for feedback, yet. You may at some later date if you need that. You're only asking them to hear it and to bear witness to this you.

Chapter 5

UNLOCKING THE CLOSET

I want to tell you something sacred and beautiful about yourself. Something true and worth remembering: every bit of you is a precious jewel that's meant to be worn and seen. Never make who you are a prison unto yourself. You have a dark and delicious nature, a way of being that starts a fire in the world. Like the Original Story and Medicine that are your air, your dark nature is your fire. Your fire forged great jewels that you must wear, jewels that are worn with such humility and confidence that they become a prismatic representation of you. You may have found that your medicinal properties include being the priestess of power or truth. Maybe you expand peace simply by being present. Or you may have found that your creative eye knows how to arrange a space to invite in comfort and curiosity.

Let yourself wander with excitement into the closet where you have stored all the pieces of you. These are your soul. They are the jewels of your dark nature that were shoved and thrown into this tiny, dark space. These are what make you dangerously necessary. The dangerous woman is the one who will not be messed with. She is the one who will take a stand for the right of all that must be, including regaling herself with her dark nature. The dangerous one teaches courage and how to love with wild abandon. The dangerous ones will show the world how to take the leap of faith that changes everything. Your dark nature will have you take a stand for your humanity. Those who fear their jewels wander lost in the fog of unlived potential. As you wear your jewels, you tell people who you are. Your name is among these jewels. Your medicine heals, in part, because it shows you in your own nature. Your dark and dangerous jeweled nature is the permission you have waited for from others. Those who wear their nature are a force to be reckoned with. They are determined to walk in the world in love and with their wild nature. They lead the world by example.

Don't be afraid of what is dark and dangerous. This is danger redefined. Danger here is that which heals and calls for all healing. Danger in this context is *I am the one who knows who I am. I am undeterred in my truth and love of all humanity.* Here your clarity is a danger to the larger society and of the ego that preys on the weak-minded. In the dark and dangerous cavern, you belong to all this beautiful universe, and as one who belongs you walk the determined path of love. The dark nature is where we go to hear the truth of our ancestors. When my people crawl into the *innipi* to pray it is dark inside. It is the womb of Mother Earth. We are held in a nurturing nature. There is a lovely invitation of the dark to know oneself away from the shields and swords. The dark invites us to let everything go so we can rediscover the aspects of our nature that we have denied and suppressed; it's a dance with sheer vulnerability. We go inside to talk to Mother Earth and to pray. In the darkness we sing our songs, and it is in this life of prayer, in the dark, that we torch the fire within that brings light. We leave not only cleansed, but also with insights and initiatives we otherwise wouldn't have had.

You will become intimate with your fire, your wild and naughty and amazingly creative nature, if you give it the comfort of the dark caverns it craves. There's no need to be afraid of your dark nature. It is not something that needs managing. It needs freedom and space to support your certain evolution. There are compelling visions there. There are incredible insights there. Go deep. Go dark and find the jewels and wear them well.

The Safety and the Closet

The closet is that place where your dark nature is sent when it is deemed a nuisance to others. When you're shy about showing it, your confidence leaves and your jewels follow. It's where you store the rarest parts of yourself, taking them out only when you feel safe to expose your fire. Until now. It's the humor that dared people and was deemed inappropriate when it should have been regarded as healing and freeing, as your soul intended. It's the deep passion that had you speak on behalf of the unseen, the poor, the gay, the mentally ill, the people of color. Your passion was told, "That's nice, darling, but it's too much and we are doing the best we can." It's your no-bullshit meter that was stomped on until it was shattered. It's your poetry that was deemed cute but not relevant in the capitalist world. It's your insights that scared others.

Why do we listen to the rants of the ones who are afraid? Because they speak so loud that they drown out the voice within. That is, until the day we become clear about our voice; that day we become dangerous. When you become dangerous you do not protect your nature; you unleash it. The idea of protection is born from the ego. It works diligently to make you believe that you need protection, which instills an unconscious sense of fear within. Love knows nothing of protection because it is unnecessary.

Now that you have your story and know your medicine it's time to weave in all the other precious parts of you. It's time to walk in total congruence and to be at home with yourself. People desire peace, self-confidence, and freedom, and they believe they need to work to attain them. But they are not something one goes out to get. Peace and its cousins are what you hold within you. You access them when you are willing to express those qualities every day. When you free them, wear them, and live them, you will *become* them. You are peace. You are freedom. You are joy. You are love. If you say so, then it shall be. We will believe what you behave.

Perhaps you were instructed to pause these precious pieces and you stowed them away, believing they were negative. Perhaps you were left feeling you needed to "be better" or "be good enough." And so you waited, and the jewels waited, until all was clear and it was safe to emerge. Be clear, now, that you and only you can make it safe to emerge. Safety doesn't arrive on your doorstep like a neatly wrapped package. Safety is never something someone else gives you, completely. Someone can make us feel safe to be or do a thing for a moment, but ultimately we hammer out our own definition of safety. This is how we discover our bravery gene. Live dangerously free. This is not the kind of danger that will cost you anything. There is nothing to fear here. Danger is your safety. You are only dangerous to your ego and the societal ego that believes behaving and conforming are required. Danger knows another way and it's liberating.

Open the door of your mind. As you do this, grant yourself the freedom from the desire to be safe. Unlocking your closet swaths you in freedom. Permission doesn't happen with one toe in the water. No one takes a leap of faith in two jumps. That's why it's called *a* leap. Its instructions are clear. It's a full-on baptismal dunk in the deep end of the water called *love thyself.* You being your whole dark, dangerous, and beautiful self brings you and others around you the safety you desire. Yes, there will be jobs, marriages, friends, and situations that will be affected, but did you think you were safe playing small there? Did you believe that love was negotiable, based on you playing small and hiding away your jewels? Were you really loved for yourself? Or were you loved for the compromises you were willing to make? No more of that. How about we eliminate the games of playing hide-and-seek with your magnificent nature? You are dark and dangerous. And you are beautiful. Be here with all you are.

Protect Your Jewels

I was engaged to a man who had chased me for 10 solid years. He charmed me and said all the right things. After a decade, I said yes. I believed his charm and his love. As soon as he felt he had attained me, his charms fell away and he picked up a dagger to try to rob me of my jewels. My nature, which he had found so alluring, was suddenly something he wanted to kill. When I asked him how a skirt looked on me, his reply was, "It shows the good half of your leg." When I admired myself in a new bra with my ample bosom, he chimed in, "More than a handful is a waste." When I came home and found a postcard from an ex-girlfriend of his on the coffee table, he laughed, saying, "Oh, that's just a private joke between her and me." When I finally broke up with him, his departing words were, "You should love yourself more." What he was really saying was, "You can't love yourself if you are with me." He knew that he was, as my Dinè brother Fabian called him, a fox, a trickster, an unworthy one. No one gets to pause or possess your jewels. What I failed to trust was the 10 years of saying no to him and my own intuitive knowing. I compromised my dark, jeweled nature when I said yes—until I didn't say yes anymore.

No one gets to douse your fire with their toxic water. Others may admire your dark, jeweled nature. Admirers shall remain acquaintances, for their gaze is never to be confused with love, which draws us near to give more of itself. Admirers are just that: they admire your flame but are not ready to fan their own flame. You are beautiful with your dark and dangerous nature. Keep it close to you. Share it, sure, but don't build a fire for someone who is not willing to chop their own wood.

The Art of Being a Firekeeper

Our jewels can be dark, fierce, and seemingly dangerous, but what appears dangerous to another is the thing that cares for what is most precious for all. It is only dangerous in the hands of someone who doesn't know how to tend their fire or is too timid to care for it. Your dark, dangerous, and beautiful nature isn't a nefarious danger to be feared. It is the spark that lights the fire that brings us close to one another. Your fire challenges your ego and expands your consciousness. Your fire is compassed by your soul and no other can tell you how to tend to it.

I've watched my elders build fires with such attention one would presume there was something human in that bundle of wood. The trees are our ancient ones who speak their own language of wisdom as they burn. The Firekeeper lays each log with care, praying the entire time. The Firekeeper never leaves the fire once it's started. She is the keeper of the trees' wisdom. Firekeeping is a ceremony in itself. The Firekeeper tends to it like a newborn, always making sure it's fed and ablaze. For the sweat lodge there are stones heating in the fire, preparing themselves to hold our prayers and tears and to cleanse us. As we prepare for the ceremony we make an offering of tobacco to the flame and what it holds, praying for whatever is in our hearts.

You, too, have a flame, and it is firing up your unique dark nature. As the keeper of this flame of dark and dangerous beauty, you must make yourself an offering to the world. Give your fire a way to warm us. If you are the one who tells the truth, be the truth teller with fiery love and compassion. If you are the one who holds the circle for others to belong, trust this is your circle to create and hold. Stop questioning whether you are doing it correctly. Stop training with others to learn more. If you need more instruction the fire will tell you. If you are the orator with a message of divine inquiry, speak in full voice with no parameters about how and where; every place is your platform. If you are the one who calls us to our highest self, be that unequivocally. Yes, your fire is dangerously sacred. Not everyone will come close. But no one can find you if your flame is not lit. Don't wait until you have taken enough courses. Don't wait for the academic abbreviations after your name—the Ph.D. or M.B.A. or M.F.A.—to speak for your validity. Don't minimize your fire for the safety of others. Don't wait. Be an earnest and present Firekeeper. Everyone has fire. What you need to grow will be shown as you live your path. We are not everything at once. Sure, good intentions may not be enough, so get your elder and mentors to support you. Not everyone learns how to build their fire or how to pray to it and dance with it. But no one who dances on this earth dances without their internal fire blazing brightly.

The Dark Naming

Being dark gets a bad name. Everything dark is dangerous, suspicious, and without light. Who, then, would want to associate with the dark side? Dark is to be rebuked. But you have been offered another view of the beauty of your dark nature. When one is searching for their purpose, they may look past the door labeled "dark and dangerous." There is risk in being you, but there is certain death in not being you. What you have to give and be in part comes from your dark and fiery nature. And because of its nature and the courage required to embrace it, many walk right past the dark and dangerous door searching for something easier to be with than the dark within. The one who will be named lives arm in arm with courage. Your name doesn't gift you with courage, it gifts you with the reason to have courage—the courage to live as only you can and as only you should. Living your divine mandate is what you are here to do. Open up into the dark nature and glorify your life. Your dark nature is an ancient and wise voice that resists the call of perfection, conformity, or someone else's standard for how you *should* be in this world. Your dark nature holds the boundary that no one dare cross. The one who holds the dark is the one who dares to speak up when others pretend nothing corrupt has occurred. The holders of the dark love boldly, change courageously, and innovate and invite wildly.

Cultures and societies tell a woman how many children she should have, whether she should work or not, paint or not, speak or not, even think or not. These edicts and ideas are insidious suggestions for how a woman should be; they are not your thoughts, your ideas, your dreams, or your nature. For men, it's how manly, how athletic, how smart, and how rich they should be, not to mention how many women they should bed in their life. Distinguishing your dark nature from all the edicts of society will keep you steady on *your* path. Your wild, dark, and often dangerous nature is where you learn how to define your reality. It is your texture.

In a recent session with a new client, Mairi, I asked, "So what is it you're wanting to birth into the world?"

Mairi replied, "I don't know."

"Tell me about what is rich in you," I prodded.

"I don't know."

I sighed. "Mairi," I said, "I'm going to be direct with you. You don't have time for the evasion of your soul. You know what is rich, sacred, and dangerous about you, so share that now. Life is too short to give me the shovel to do your digging when only you can say what's true. This is your life. Don't you want to live it?"

"Yes," she replied.

"Well then," I said. "What is your dark nature that you're willing to admit to?"

I could hear her chest expand with an inhale as she prepared to let herself out of prison. It was as though she were giving herself the breath of life that she had not breathed before. She might have also called me a few names here. I was challenging her to move now, without the months of warm-up time her fear was asking of her. It was time to leap and just say, "Fuck it."

Then Mairi spoke: "I love the discourse of challenge, not for the sake of argument but for the sake of opening our minds to each other. I want deep conversations to reign." She was clearly tired of the cocktail conversation of "What do you do for a living?"

"Mairi, this is how you make love in the world!" I told her. "Now that you admit you're pregnant, let's make plans for a brilliant birth."

Perhaps you think that I was rough with her. Yes, I was a bit handy with Mairi. There's a time to be gentle and there's a time to be hands-on and to really grab at the clay of the heart, holding it while it speaks. Unveiling your dark nature often happens with a trembling hand and heart. You will be called to rub off all the dust that has accumulated over the years. Your first birth came at the expense of deep pain, a signal that everything was happening as it should.

I had one more question I needed to ask Mairi, and I also ask it of you now: How do you get in your own way of caring for your dark nature?

Mairi responded by asking me to help her not outsmart me. She said she can talk a good game and tell me what I want to hear and thus bypass her most essential self.

My reply? I sensed a strong, no-bull kind of woman, so I said: "Nope! I am not going to manage your brilliance that you make into an obstacle—that is your job. Our first order of work is for you to make a commitment to know your fear, your ego, and to not put me in charge of that.

It's time you became responsible for how you circumvent your nature and your life."

Loving a challenge and after cursing at being busted, Mairi agreed.

Here's the thing: if you don't earnestly admit how your fears manage the heck out of you every single day of your life, then you will forever be held hostage to the belief that your dark nature and your jewels are bad and need to be locked away. Know your obstacles and you will defeat them.

While Mairi won't be alone on her journey, the work is hers to do. How else will she become acquainted with her capacity? I will stand by her side bearing witness to the integration of her dark beauty as will your family (*family* meaning anyone who gets and loves you). You can't wait to become you. Don't wait until you are older to be free and wholly you. You might have more knowledge but you will regret the time you wasted, waiting. You'll spend your time watching others walking proudly with their jewels wishing you had yours on. You'll take courses, attend retreats, and hire coaches and therapists, when you could have just leaped. It's scary or not. It's easy or not. It's always freeing. Get up and unlock your closet!

Look in your heart and see the fire of your beauty. Hold nothing back. You may offend us—so be it. You may lose friends and jobs. It's okay. Your fire can't teach you anything about you if you douse it with water. When you light that fire, only then will it light the way to peace, self-confidence, and freedom. You may be clumsy with it at first, but fires can be relit. So light the fire, baby, and keep us all warm next to you.

The Falsity of Good, Bad, Right, and Wrong

Living with the polarity of being good and bad, right and wrong, we lock our dark nature in a closet hoping we can rid those parts that might disgrace us and cause us to be ostracized. Isn't that the contradiction? We ostracize ourselves first. Receiving ourselves as we are is the most important work we are here to do. If you're looking for a purpose, you just found it: your purpose is to own what is eccentric, weird, and fiery about you. Your purpose is also called self-love.

In the worlds of spirituality and religion, we can be stripped of our dark, sexy, sensual jewels in attempting to do "it" (whatever *it* is) correctly, not understanding that being correct is not the path of the soul. Corrections are what prisons are called. I've watched the one in yoga class getting the pose to perfection only to walk out of the class unwilling to accept her imperfections. It's not about the pose. I've seen people say the right spiritual and religious statement, follow all the rules, truly believing they are being "good" Christians or deeply spiritual only to turn around and tell someone else that who they are and the manner in which they love shouldn't be allowed. I seem to recall Jesus being quite the rule breaker. He wasn't playing the same game as everyone else. His love had no rules for us to obey. We didn't have to qualify to be forgiven and loved.

Your dark, dangerous nature keeps your childlike wonder alive and brewing. Scoff at the notion of your life being logical or linear. When you swing the door wide open, you invite creativity to introduce its nature to yours. Creativity and passion have a chaotic order that keeps the mystery alive and ever growing. With your door wide open, live in the world of the unknown, because you never know who you will become. Dark nature has its own penmanship that will erase the routine of life. Now is always a good time to honor your spiritual integrity.

The Stance to Wield Your Soul Sword

Embracing your dark nature doesn't require too much. The sword of this new life is not used for protection; it is used to cut away at obstacles. You know how to wield yourself, your whole self, now. You are not in danger of being left in the cold grip of fear now that you have your fire. You no longer have to say no to yourself. You no longer need to behave in "acceptable" ways to belong. That is what will kill the soul. Now you allow your dark nature to speak for you. As you recollect these pieces of you, your personality will humble itself, kneeling to the prayer of your highest self. This is when the door is truly unlocked. No longer confined to places too small for your human spirit, you are as free as you desire to be.

The Practice: Unlocking the Closet

Time: 30–60 minutes
Materials: journal and pen

To open the door and reclaim what makes you whole, begin unlocking your closet by naming what is dark, dangerous, and beautiful in you. It's those pieces of you that are not "normal," those ways in which you etch your uniqueness in the world. You may be crystal clear about your dark nature. If so, then get it out on the pages of your journal; get it all down.

If you've forgotten, hidden from, or narrowed your jewels, use these inquiries to uncover what you know deep down.

- What is so loud in you that it pours out of you against even your will to hold it back?

- What do you keep trying to make right rather than free?

- What do you tone down to make others feel safe?

- Where do you feel imprisoned?

- What are you waiting to be validated for?

- In what waters do you dip your toes in but never fully swim?

- Where do you get positive feedback that makes you happy and then causes you to run away?

- What do you know about your dark nature and its gift for you and humanity?

- What are your God-given talents and how do you live and/or compromise them?

- When you are all jeweled up, who will you see in the mirror?

- When you walk with your fire, what do we see and receive from you?

- What offering do you make of yourself as the jeweled one?

- How does your jeweled nature evolve others?

- What old aspect(s) of yourself will you have to destroy to allow your dark nature to emerge?

- When will you come out to play?

These aspects that you have hidden are your jewels. They were always meant to be played with, shared, adored, and honed, but instead they were cloistered away like an unwanted burden. But you do want them, don't you? That is why they were abandoned. You wanted them badly, but the power that was you when you held them scared you and others. Unlike the example in Chapter 3, where an adult says or does something to hinder your growth, the locked closet was your doing, which means it can be undone *only* by you. Isn't it wonderful to know that?

- What do you ache to brew?

- What difference will it make to you?

- What texture will you add to this glorious world?

- What were you proud of that was of your making or design?

- What will you say to your dark nature when you free it, and what do you want it to say to you?

- Who can you not help but be in the world?

- What companionship in you does it seek?

- How will you stay jeweled when fear comes knocking?

- What will courage look like in you as you step out jeweled?

- How dangerous are you willing to become with the ego and how do you know?

These are the kinds of questions for which you already know the answers. You've held back for too long. Can you not feel the ache within your bones to create, become, and give of yourself? Sometimes we just walk our entire self into the closet and slam the door, holding the knob with both hands. We look around us and we don't see freedom, so we lock our preciousness away. The freedom to be you, to be fully aligned with your highest soul self, is right here with you now. You have to say yes to it all, not just what you are comfortable with. That innate divinity that you were born with is what you will engage to know freedom.

Unlocking the closet is the beginning of witnessing your own beauty. As you respond to these prompts, what you've always known as your truth returns home. You must behold and hold your treasures. Yes, look at them. Marvel at yourself and recognize yourself. In case your ego starts to poke its thoughts in as you do this work, rest assured that this is not narcissism, it is soul honoring. You are not arrogant for beholding yourself. You behold it so easily in others. Now is the time to stand in it as a promise, and to live it as the prayer it is in the world and for yourself.

Will you hear the profundity that you bring? Each life brings this. Each life has a sacred purpose. But no life can be fully realized without total acceptance of the dark jewels.

The Practice: Kneeling with Voice at the Altar of Your Dark Nature

Time: 20 minutes
Materials: journal and pen

There is power in kneeling. When we enter the *innipi*, we do so on our knees, humbling ourselves to Mother Earth, crawling into the dark lodge to pray, to face ourselves. That going low invites the head to bow down to the sacred. Approaching your sacredness with reverence is how you say yes to you. There are many ways to kneel. Speaking with reverence is one of them. Take a moment to bow to your nature. What you recovered from the early practice of answering the prompts has given you more than enough. Write down your story in narrative form. Tell the story of who you are. You are claiming your fire. You are collecting your jewels. So spill it out and own your fiery, dark, dangerous, and beautiful nature for the good of all.

You can use these prompts to write your story of knowing, but don't be too attached to them. If you know what you know then write, dear one. Write and spill it on the page.

- What is not "normal" about you?

- What would this abnormality transform in the world?

- What does it speak out and up for?

- What does it not tolerate in you and in the world and why?

- What and who will you have to say no to so you can wear your dark nature unabashedly?

> • How will you be dangerous in caring for
>   yourself?
>
> I am gifted with _____ in
> my jeweled nature, for the purpose of fulfilling
> _____.

Soul Determination

Stay steadfast in recognizing who you are. Practice sitting with your immense self-love, self-trust, and self-knowing. Self-knowing doesn't mean that you know how your Original Medicine will blossom in you or what your Original Story will ask of you. You are not entitled to know that beforehand. Instead you know that it will blossom within you, it will nurture your nature, and it will evolve you. You know and trust that it will bring good to the universe. As you wear and live your dark nature, the fire within you will protect you from the residue of negative influences. Negative encounters may come your way, but they will not influence your being. Honor this truth in being exactly who you are.

Lighting the Fire

The process of naming is something you last through, not blast through. Continue to be with the process, keep your focus, engage your soul. Release your judgments of what comes your way. Give up filtering life through the old lenses that cannot comprehend your new context. Light your fire proudly. In honoring your whole self you deny the call to be negotiated. You deny the conflict the ego will instigate every moment of every day with your self-loving, self-knowing, soon-to-be-named higher consciousness. You cannot negate your jeweled unique nature and stop the internal conflict (also known as fear). When you stop negotiating who you are each time your ego arises—either within you or projected onto you—you become dangerous to it. This is how you begin to light the fire that will destroy destructive forces. All you have to do is be fully you. This is the definition of self-love. This is anarchy in its most positive form. Stand in your own authority and overthrow any voice that says otherwise. What does your jeweled nature stand for, or against? Know this and your way will be clear.

The Practice: Be Someone You Love

Time: 1 hour
Materials: a companion, your journal, and your brave spirit

At some point it comes down to what you are willing to do to become who you know you are. In previous practices you were advised not to share your findings too soon and to hold things close in. For this practice it's wise to get support and to have a witness. Someone who has a bucket of love, support, and appreciation for you is the best person. Choose someone who can hold your precious wild nature and laugh with you, not fear for you.

Tell them who you desire to become. Tell them how you will not move away from yourself. Opt for specificity. Here are some ways this conversation may sound:

I am becoming bolder in asking for what I am in relationships and work. I am saying no to anyone and anything that limits my being. I will be talking to my parents and saying no to any more help with money so that I can know myself as financially solvent. I refuse to emasculate myself by being dramatic, acting as if the world is against me. I'm saying yes to writing/painting/laughing/dancing on a daily basis.

I will begin to sell my art and I need your help encouraging me and connecting me with places to sell it. Would you host an event to sell my work to help me in my coming out in the world?

I am dismissing and releasing all the pain I suffered in my past. I dismiss its recurring hold on my mind and I take a stand that says I have never been persecuted so that I am now down with the past. If I dip into my old ways of speaking or acting, will you lovingly call me back by saying: "Where did you go?"

I need you to go for walks with me in nature in complete silence. Will you laugh wildly over martinis with me and not care what onlookers think? I will be changing my hair/work/clothing/vocabulary/what I read/where I go. Stay with me as I evolve and love me as I am. I want to do a burning-the-old-and-welcoming-the-new ceremony. Will you attend?

Be brave to ask for what you need, but only ask those you know can hold you.

Ask for what you need from them. Listen to any reasonable cautions from them. They are worthy of your trust. Accept all the support that is given. Let them hold you.

In lighting the fire it's time to take a specific action that concretizes and affirms you. It's time to do the one thing that is yours to do. That one action that is a complete yes to who you know you are. It should be big enough to hold you. Your action should be big enough that it's like a good yoga stretch that lets you know you're in the game but not so stretched that you go limp for a week. It is a leap-worthy action but it is not so big that it is more for effect. For some of you it may require a plan with a few steps, but even a plan has some leap-worthy action it can take right now. For the habitual planners, planning is off the table for you, because planning is what you do to feel in control and feel safe. This is not a throw-caution-to-the-wind moment. It's a *You've thought about it enough to know that you want it* moment. Before you leap, here is a prayer for the brave-hearted ones.

Dear Brave One, the one who lives a passionate life, may you know you are surrounded by forces of good to support you.

Dear Precipice, the Brave One stands on your bluff willing to leap into the unknown. Hold her/him with grace. Tell her/him often after her/his leap and walk forward that she/he can and will do this.

Dear Child of God(dess), you walk not alone. Look up at us, the Star Nation. We are listening and will guide you. Hand over what trembles in your heart and we will clear it, returning to you a constellation of wisdom to carry you forward. We have the greatest vantage point in Father Sky. We speak often with Mother Moon and what she tells us makes us swoon. They share their great wisdom and that wisdom has withstood the ages. We are ageless and knowing. We are caring and insightful. We are family. Speak with us often.

Dear Enlightened One, stand tall as you take your next steps. Not as false bravado but as an earnest wearing of bravery. Ask for what you need when you have landed safely and you will be guided by your own wisdom and intuition. Remember to be grateful for your ability to leap. Most others jump up and down but never cross into new territory.

Dear Beautiful Soul, remember the prayer of the Beauty Way—beauty below, above, and within. Greet each day with a joyous spirit that when you rise each day you do so to meet yourself anew, never knowing what new fortitude and

*determination you will be asked to give but always be at the
ready. There will be many days you will be asked to receive
the many gifts from this universe. Do so with equal joy.*

*Dear Lover, share your love with strangers and family
alike. Give yourself like the rain does to the soil. Never with-
holding or measuring your love. You understand love now.
You know love doesn't leave you vulnerable. Love is vulnerable. You understand now that loving doesn't require you to
be in harm's way. You understand that the omnipresence of
your love can be felt and given from any place at any time.
Proximity thinking belongs to those who still believe time
and space are real.*

*Dear One, you have the poem of your soul sewn into
you, like the ink of a tattoo, it is stained in beauty all over
you. You know who you are. You know what is needed. Face
forward with pride and step on.*

The prayer is complete. Move forward in your leap
with faith and with your trusted companion.

The Practice: Being You

Time: 5 minutes
Materials: recorder or smartphone

Record what you did and what you experienced.
Now rest. This is more than enough.

Chapter 6

A LITTLE LESSON IN PASSION AND CURIOSITY

You have passion. The word *passion* often gets confused with the word *desire*.

Desire means to wait for something. We often use "desire" when we mean "want." Desire is actually more closely related to the word *longing*, which means to yearn for something or someone.

Your desires lead you to open doors that you might not have considered. Desire takes you to doors that need closing or nailing shut. When the ego gets hold of your desires it can also lead you to doors that destroy you. You've got fire. You can use it to bring light to something or you can use it to burn something to the ground. In either case, take great care building your fire. Light or ashes—both are worthy of your respect.

While you might have to wait for a desire to materialize, passion acts like a magnet pulling you toward the things you are meant to be intimately close with. Passion puts your heart on center stage. Your mind agrees with its directives. You can't help going forward. Passion is tough to resist because it's based in a soul calling. Passion can feel like lust but with a happier ending. Originally passion was associated with the Passion of Christ and was defined as suffering. Today we define passion as a strong and barely controllable urge to be, do, or experience something of ourselves. When you are not aligned or doing your right work in the world, that would most certainly cause you suffering. In Chapter 4, you were asked to consider the question, What is your air? What can you *not* do in this world? The answer would describe your passion in life. Passion often gives way to purpose. It invokes your medicine. Passion is relevant for you and your naming because your name should call you into an experience of yourself and the world as a unique venture. This is why it is important not to be beholden to structures to keep you safe or believe in normalcy as a personal destination. Passion cannot, without substantial suffering, squeeze itself into the grayness of "normal" that the large society would like. There is more for you that is distinctly different from the "more" the larger society wants you to be. Society's version of more is not internal; it is external, materialistic. Society's version is not based in passion or curiosity, but rather in a lack of self-love. This vision creates a hole in you that can never be filled.

If you don't know what you are passionate about, look into your medicine bundle. What in your medicine is underused? What does your medicine want to show you about how you look at the world?

When you look at something you've seen a hundred times or listen to someone tell a story you've already heard, instead of being bored, look for God in it. God is ever present, attempting to show the unwavering beauty of the world. Get into a "seeing beyond the veil" mode of being incredibly curious. How did that come to be? Boredom represents a lack of engagement. Because we are rewarded for what we know, thinking on our feet, maintaining a routine, we may believe that there is power in this. It can give the false illusion and desire for safety—as though safety were something we should want.

In opening yourself to passion it's also necessary to get out of your tiny, too-tight box. Start to read magazines and books you've avoided because they don't appeal to your politics, religion, and so on. Be truly curious. Argue with the literature if you like, but stay curious. Curiosity is the portal to the love of imagination. You will need your imagination not only to be named, but also to navigate the rest of your life. You are free to imagine your life anew each day. Each morning when you rise, you can sit with yourself and ask the all-knowing to guide you. Each day is a new region within and without for you to draw upon. Ask the soul within: What do you have for me today?

In a world full of logistics, passion can go unattended when we are young, waiting for us to settle into ourselves. As we age, we come to understand that passion is self-care. Caring for the soul self takes time and attention that we don't always give ourselves. Some just seem to know or are somehow introduced to their passion from the womb, while others bump into their passion along their path. And for some it takes the rite of passage to saying yes too often to the wrong things and the wrong people before they let go of life to find their passions.

If you are 20 to 30 years old and passion has eluded you, you have been playing the straight and narrow for too long. I see so many young ones just trying to find their way—trying to find the "right" career, the "right" love, and the "right" version of themselves. Or they are just following the rules to be accepted. The rules can be made by parents, religious leaders, educational institutions, and workplaces. I have noted before how society's rules of your value as a woman are indicated by how sexual and beautiful you are, that your body should look a certain way and that a man is the determinant of your beauty. I have seen men wandering through life looking for someone to lead them into manhood instead of looking within. When we don't look within to the voice of our own godliness, our identity is up for grabs. Our natural state of curiosity is corrupted and our passion is exchanged for lust. We don't challenge. We don't opt out. Stop for an hour each day and wonder what more life is trying to show you. Remember to wonder. Wonder a little more each day.

You're taking a risk to move out of societal rules and into freedom. As a Named One you are daring your ego, society's ego, to try to stop you. The risk is not that you won't make it to the other side as you follow your soul. The risk is in the beginning, when you're about to leap, when you're standing on the precipice of staying in control and looking at the distance to living in freedom; that's when there's a risk that you might turn your back on the bluff and tell yourself, *It's too windy today, I'll try tomorrow.* The risk is that you'll say no to yourself. Perhaps you will do something shocking to feel something different from the nothing you are stuck in. Instead, do something that rips open your passionate self. Pull at the threads of your passions. Go out into the world, into your community, all the while listening for passion and curiosity to speak. They will. They always do. Get out of your regular circles and go sit and listen to the stories of older people.

Oh, the 40-year-olds. You have the itch. This is the time to scratch. You've played by the rules. You birthed and cared for your children. You worked and made your mark, or perhaps you never ventured out completely. Your body of work lies right over there, in a dark drawer where no light can see it; it's in your heart but perhaps you've never brought it to your mind. You have found and lost love, and perhaps found it again. You have spent 40 years on this planet but you have not reaped its teachings in full. Now is your time to be unequivocally rude to your life and to strip it down. Yes, be rude to the voices that have laid down smooth roads in your mind that question all your passion and curiosity. Rest assured that your children will eat. Rest assured that if you didn't have children that you made the right choice and can still have a child some way if you so desire. Rest assured that you will remain lovable to those who want your passion to rule, in your rude awakening.

If you're 50, 60, 70, or 80-plus years old, chances are high that you know darn well what your passions are. Society might be telling you that you are invisible. Let me tell you for a fact that your visibility is more apparent and vibrant than the larger society could ever see. See your gray hair and your folding skin as the wisdom that has taken five decades to etch into you. You are radiant. Your body may not have the agility of a 20-year-old, oh but your mind has become so agile you can bend what we believe is certain reality. Now shake off the dust that has settled, pretending to tell you that if you move it will fall to the ground. No! You are the keeper of great love and passion for life. Stand up! If you haven't touched your wild ambitions, your desires, your curious ideas, now is the time for you to dust off that box and go make serious love with what you've always loved. If you don't know the how of it, go hang out with groups who are doing what they love. I spy every weekend at my local coffee shop a group of women knitters. I love sitting next to them, listening to them talk about what they are doing. Do I knit? NO! Will I knit? NO! And yet I love listening to and feeling their passion. I am inspired by how fully they give themselves to their needles and yarn. I watch the experienced knitters guiding the newbies, and I sense the love of their art and of one another. It encourages me to give myself to my art and to guide others with theirs. These women are teaching me about how passion gives way to incredible creativity. I'm learning how to embrace passion. Go find passionate people who will inspire you. The how is not the steps of what to do next. The how is what vibrant energy will you bring to your desires?

Your desire to be named is in part a desire to know or be reunited with your passion. In unlocking the closet and recovering your jeweled dark nature you are reunited with your fiery nature. A precious stone like a sapphire is mounted in something strong enough, worthy enough to hold it, like gold or titanium. Your dark jewels are mounted in passion, compassion, love, and faith. You can now get on with your work in the world. I say *work* because it will be something you do over the course of your lifetime with this new sturdy hold of love, passion, compassion, and faith. This is how all work was meant to be. Passion will support your undying focus and care. Make a practice of feeling into your passion. Hold it in your chest and feel your love for it. Touch the paintbrushes as you pass them.

This is also what makes you dangerous because it is this passion within that you will not let die. You will protect it because it is the giver of life and because it breathes beauty into you and the world. Hold on to your passion. Don't allow circumstances to pry it loose. The Named One walks with their jewels set in a beautiful design of passion. Remember that what you desire may not always be what you need, but what you need, as a spiritual one, will be given to you with passion. It is a life-giving force and fire-starting energy that will support the leaps over your future precipices. Not every day is bright. Not every day is dark. But every day you have a fire that you can warm to. It is called your passion. Get a match!

The Practice: Listen to the Call of Beauty

Time: 30–60 minutes
Materials: music, access to nature, and, later, your journal

Listen! To call up your passion and your curiosity, I ask you to listen to something beautiful.

Take the time to go out to the forest, and as you walk cup your ear to hear the sounds you may not ordinarily notice as you walk and look around. Stop on the path, cup your ear with one hand, and listen deeply. Let the sound into your heart. You don't need to understand it. You don't need to identify it. Notice what it brings into you. What does it sing into you?

In winter, listen to a beautiful passage of music without lyrics. A piece of music that transports you into a land you have never visited. Let it take you on a tour of yourself. Allow yourself to listen from your chest rather than your ears.

Remember your passion and the curiosity and imagination it preserved. That manuscript you started that has not been touched by you or read by others. The yarn you purchased, the tap dancing shoes you bought, the memo you drafted but never submitted to the company. Your passions will wait patiently for you, but why would you want to create unconscious suffering for yourself? Step into your heart and reintroduce yourself to your passion. Aren't you curious about what it wants to say and do? If you are thinking, *but I'm frightened*, did you think you wouldn't be? Don't you think most people who move forward are frightened? They are!

Robert Heller said, "Fear is excitement without breath." Fear is part of the deal. You have to give more attention, more care, more faith to your passion than to your fear. Breathe. Touch your work. Do your art.

Chapter 7

THE COUNCIL OF ELDERS

With all the internal landscaping you have done it is time for some external support. In the Native tradition, we are supported through storytelling and other conversations around the fire, before and during a ceremony. Often our elders will receive us for a visit, or they will come to see us, especially if they know we are at a critical point on our path or are suffering. We ask our elders for help and offer them tobacco; if they accept, the mentoring begins. In the non-Native world I'm not sure how most people get supported; so many are afraid to ask for help. They feel they are a burden and never bother to give the gift to another—the opportunity to be supportive. Most people would love to help you; it feels so good to know we are needed. But receiving help is frowned upon in Western cultures. When you look at indigenous peoples around the world, we all work in community. None of us would ever think of ourselves as an island or a burden. Community offers that holy communion that gives to one another. The Council of Elders is an incredible circle of wisdom that is available to us in addition to the support we already have or as a base of support if we don't have that kind of circle around us.

My elders Pablo and Andrea live in New Mexico, and years after I left that state to return home to California, I felt very alone. I didn't attend any ceremonies or have any conversations with Native people. I was starting my business and traveling the world speaking. I was alone and hungry for the kind of conversations and leadership I'd had before. I loved the power of meditation, but I needed the conversation as well. So I brought my elders to the living room in my mind.

Believing that people are never gone—that they may be unseen but are always available to us—I created my own Council of Elders. You can use this Council of Elders practice to step forward in your naming process and in your bigger life as the Named One. Having walked between the two worlds of spirit and earth, as Shorty noted in his artwork on my pipe, I knew the power of going into the great beyond. I knew my elders and their wisdom were with me if only I called on them and listened well. Now as I do my morning gratitude, I thank all my elders and ancestors who have gone before me but are still providing me their continued guidance, love, and support. I then call in my sacred grandmothers for blessings and guidance. I believe that at any time we each can access what Carl Jung called the collective unconscious. I don't think Dr. Jung was thinking of my grandmothers as the collective unconscious when he introduced the term, but I believe we can form a version of it that works for us.

You'll need your passion to light the ceremonial fire to host your Council of Elders. This is a visioning practice that you can do easily every day to receive guidance and support. You may think as you do your visualization that you are making it up . . . and that's okay—you are! You are calling in the spirits. You are using your mind as a channel for their wisdom and yours.

Make an altar of your mind and alter your world.

Have Faith

In the previous chapter you were invited to evoke your passion with a reminder that it is your passion that will be the fire that you and your elders will circle around. As you honor the power of love, compassion, and faith, you will come to know your interdependence and responsibility for all humanity. These powers will support your own growth and enlightenment, where your consciousness will expand how you walk in this life. This is no burden; it is freeing.

Before you go into the practice, I want to take you on a tour of faith, as it will be an integral part of your named life. In *The Barnhart Concise Dictionary of Etymology*, the word *faith* is defined as "loyalty and allegiance." If you have to be loyal and give your allegiance to something, let it be love. Have faith in the truth that you are loved. Trust that love is guiding you. You will learn the value of walking with and in the faith of love. Faith is an absolute trust and confidence that you are supported in this earthly realm to be and do *you* precisely as you are. You must listen well to your heart, to your soul, and to the elders, as they are aligned with your highest self. Faith can take immense courage because it really is putting one sturdy foot on a path that has not been paved. You are cutting a new path in the world. Your new world is still unknown and as such, faith is your best companion. Others may be doing something or being someone similar to you, but they are not you. They have their path to chart and you have yours. Faith is the strong rope you hang on to as your world is being built or falling away. The one who stands in faith knows well what it is like to trust in the unseen, while others point and scoff or run away in fear. Faith is tending to your garden knowing spring is coming. Faith is a teacher of patience. It is a steadfast practice that softens the heart space for others and thus teaches the faithful one to have compassion and love for others. You know the road is not always easy, but it is good. Faith is a spiritual practice. Faith does not mean you sit on your yoga cushion all day chanting "om" or attend ceremonies and do nothing more. Faith will move you into action. It will shut your mouth when words are not enough or dare you to speak a word of resonance, trusting in the power of one powerful word. Faith will say yes when the world is leaning into no. It will say stay when your ego says leave. Faith will put you on bended knee to humble you if your ego takes over. It will eradicate worry. It will discriminate against chance and foster opportunity. It will make a prayer of you. Be faithful to your visions and your passion. Faith is your elder—let it teach you.

Move into passion and faith now as you prepare yourself for your first Council of Elders. Ask for whatever guidance you need. If you feel nothing is coming from the session you can be sure that the doubt of the ego is near. Ask your elders to move doubt aside so you can hear them.

The Practice: Gathering Your Elders

Time: 30–60 minutes
Materials: a recorder and your journal

Before you begin the practice spend some time considering what kind of elder wisdom you want and which elders would embody it. Take a few moments to vision those people. You are determining who you bring into the circle of fire. Some may want all women elders. You may want to bring past family members along with unknown elders. Instead of humans, your elders may be in the form of energy. Or they may be a mixture of humans and energy. Once you are clear on who you are inviting, start the practice below.

As with all the practices, make sure you have undisturbed time. I give myself 30 minutes to one hour. You can do less, maybe just 20 minutes to start. I promise you'll be so engaged you will want more time.

Prepare as if for a meditation. Light a candle to represent the fire and breath. When you're ready, see in your mind's eye—the space between your eyebrows—a fire. Picture this fire in your perfect location outdoors. Outdoors all the elements are always represented.

Send a belly breath to the top of your head and open your mind.

When you feel your mind opening and being receptive, tap the top of your head with your middle finger. Lightly tap, tap.

Continue to breathe and open up your heart space. It is with your heart that you call in your elders.

Using your middle finger, tap your heart area twice: tap, tap.

Good, now breathe down into your belly a big breath, holding the intake and slowly releasing the breath. You will take into your body what is said. Inhale and exhale once more and with your middle finger tap your belly twice.

Calling in the Wisdom

Sit comfortably and respectfully and see your circle in your mind's eye. See the bright flame calling in wisdom, including yours. Your wise elders will gather in this circle. Take in the place where you are holding this circle. Breathe that location in. It's important to you.

I call in two groups of elders, my grandmothers from beyond and my Native elders who I do not get to see. Often elders I've never known show up, too. You can decide to focus on a kind of energy you want present and see who shows up. Whoever comes is attending in love and grace. In your way, with your words, invite your elders to the circle, knowing that everyone you have in heart and mind will come forward. They always do.

See them in the circle. However they appear is right for you. Begin by thanking them for being there with you today. Start your conversation. Listen well. Take note of their presence, how they speak to you, and what words they use to convey their wisdom. These are your teachers. Pay close attention—school is in session and you are supported here. Notice how you are being held in love. Notice as you listen what you are learning about who you want to become as you walk as the Named One. Their presence will teach you as much as their words.

Completion

Completion is about honoring one another. It's not serving up platitudes or flowering up the truth. It's saying, *It's time to say good-bye for now, thank you, and here is how you impacted me*. Most people don't take the time to complete a relationship, particularly if it isn't going well. Imagine what could be different if we took time to thank the people in our lives, even when it's time to say good-bye. Most church rituals close with "Amen." Natives close with "Mitakuye Oyasin" and a handshake. Here you are using completion to honor your elders. In this ceremony it's important to grace your Council of Elders with gratitude. After years of tutelage we do a giveaway ceremony in which we gift our elders as a way of saying thank you.

Completion is a ceremony, and when you hold people with reverence and speak in gratitude for all, they will hear whatever you say. When you are ready, in your own way thank them for being there with you. You may decide to bow to them. Find your way to close this time, knowing you can come back whenever you desire.

I encourage you to return to this practice daily and watch your sense of self become rooted in confidence, trust, and faith—not to mention the self-respect you acquire. These are your jewels. Wear them.

Chapter 8

EVOCATIVE WORD
RESONANCE

Meeting with your elders gives you new information, true belonging, and support that will aid you on your journey. You'll need a new language to speak your wisdom into the world. The realm of honoring your story, medicine, and nature requires a language as beautiful, evocative, provocative, and sensual as the world you now live in. Language and the words that make up language are incredibly powerful. In the world of data, technology, and social media, we are taught to abbreviate our life force. The growth of technology has created something that has never happened before: we are being asked to move at light speed, to reply to messages, to post on our social media outlets, and to respond to other posts—right now. In a whirlwind of moving fast we can easily pick up the debris of casualness in how we approach each soul, without even noticing. Some of the debris that has been swept along is the belief that brevity is what people want. We've become a society that desires shortcuts. It tells us we do not have an attention span greater than a gnat. It is not that our attention span has been abbreviated, it's that we don't know what we should pay attention to so we give our attention to everything. The fear of being left out of something incredible has taught us to be a part of everything, because anything could be relevant. Such is the experience of a young technology. We are not listening to one another anymore, because we are not saying anything with depth and resonance.

When you speak to someone, practice being conscious about what you are sending them. Do you remember the children's rhyme "Sticks and stones may break my bones but words will never hurt me"? If you've ever been called something that made you feel small, you know how untrue it is. Words heal and grow, and they also hurt and wound us.

As you worked through Chapter 3 ("Childhood Interrupted"), you probably recalled many wounding things that were said to you when you were young. You have also experienced the validating vibration of being verbally loved. Your life doesn't need abbreviation. It needs you to surrender to one full experience at a time, instead of as many as you can gather. This is the meaning of "quality, not quantity." In this chapter, you will be introduced to powerful words that will give your listeners "ear love." You will speak words the soul misses. These simple yet complex words, when used consistently, expand your consciousness and deepen your relationships. When you use words that are *intended* solely for the purpose of evoking your highest nature—love—you become what you say. Being conscious of the words you use is not about being careful about what you say. When you speak with consciousness, you need never be concerned with being politically correct; you don't have to walk on eggshells trying to say the most pleasing or nicest thing. That's crafting conversation for an end in mind that serves the speaker not the listener. Resonant words are gifts of seeing others and wanting to be present with them. Consciousness knows what it is doing; it doesn't need help or filters. It *is* the help and the filter.

The Named One has learned to say no to what is not hers. She takes time to speak with intention, to hear what her new vocabulary wants to say to herself and to others. Language has its own landscape and its own texture. It creates a specific scenery and touch points into which the listener is invited to participate. The words that make up sacred language provide a texture of intensity, intimacy, richness, and fire, and that engages curiosity, wonder, and imagination. Yes, the topography of word resonance is one of vast imagination and creativity. It is the *namaste* (I bow to you) of the speaking world.

You can speak words that represent your soul's intention and simultaneously silence the ego mania. When you speak a soul-resonant language it swaddles your soul and your ego. Your soul bows to resonant language as a greeting of a long-lost friend. Whenever love is present, the ego has nowhere to go and nothing to say. Love soothes even the ego, giving it an opportunity to pause itself.

The Power of Speaking Resonant Words

When our vocabulary becomes a prayer, we speak one word at a time. We know that our mind has loosened the shackles of the prison we've made of it. Words have an intention that creates an energetic obligation that will be lived. We say things and have no idea of the impact we are having. You are already experiencing this. When you use disclaimers about your power it's harder to invoke it. When you misuse your humility by speaking small about yourself, your mind hears everything as true. A friend was laughing at a comedian and turned to me, saying, "I love self-deprecation, it makes him seem human." Isn't that sad that we need others to express self-disapproval in order to relate? Such are the antics of the ego—it makes us believe that this is humility. When you make hyperbolic statements, it takes you high but eventually crashes you hard on the pavement of its needy extravagance.

Words represent us in a way that nothing else does. We are constantly sharing with others who we are, what we believe, and what we value by what we say and how we say it—or by what we don't say. We are speaking a melodic story that writes the path we walk and invites the listener to walk with us or to run fast in the other direction. The casualness or dramatic use of language can create a chaotic melody that spins you into a frenetic tale of drama.

When we agree to represent our highest self and our highest truth, we learn to deepen our vocabulary to accurately represent this truth. When we speak with resonant language, we invite evolution, enlightenment, grace, and beauty to be a part of us. We invite these qualities in and welcome their wisdom; their medicinal properties become a part of our being.

Being named is not magical; it is not a sparkling fairy tale. It is grounded in ancient wisdom. Names that are recognized and those given in ceremony are given with the wisdom's directive imparted. At the end of Vickie's Original Story in Chapter 4, she shares her name: "All that belongs to me." You can feel the resonance come off the page. Her name creates a resonance that she will never be apart from. Naming aligns you with your soul's natural evolutionary process. Giving a language to your reality with words that vibrate at a higher level supports your named evolution.

Mapping Desires

I've coached people all over the world; often they are all seeking the same three experiences of themselves:

1. They want to live with meaning and purpose (a.k.a, living as the Named One).

2. They desire more peace and less inner struggle.

3. They desire more personal freedom to be who they are without apology. (Sometimes the third desire is framed as happiness or living their dream.)

These are worthy desires when they are cultivated within us. The outward search to possess distracts us from the treasures within. Meaning and purpose, peace, personal freedom, and happiness all live within. The fact that people do not experience them is not because they don't have them; it's because they don't have *access* to them. Most people believe they will be happy when X, Y, or Z happens. But this is an illusion of our making that spins the exhausting nightmare of more seeking. A way out of the nightmare and illusion is to turn away from the idea that there is a *search* and instead think of it as *journey* within, an exploration of how you will speak your reality into being. Living as someone who is on a journey is radically different from living as someone who is always searching. Searching engages longing, which is created from a belief or an experience that you do not have what you want. A journey is responding to the call of your soul to see rather than seek. Each high-resonance word spoken prompts a new behavior, a new way of thinking for the person speaking it.

Certain Death

The journey asks you to allow your Original Story to speak itself into you and to walk in your Original Medicine. The journey is not easy, but it is no struggle. It will uplift, not exhaust. The journey will ask you to shed old skin for new. That is both joyous and often painful when we resist or fear change. Why are we so afraid of change? We grew up from childhood to adulthood without much resistance. Was this because it simply happened to us and to those around us, so we unconsciously accepted physical growth as normal? But what we cannot see we challenge, resist, or deny. Change and transformation are a part of your process. Yes, emotional and spiritual growth ask more than mere physical growth, as the latter happens without your input. But we should jump for joy at the fact that we have input when it comes to our spiritual growth. This should be celebrated, not feared. You sign up for and sign off on everything you want to experience. You do it consciously. You are that powerful. That is cause for constant celebration. The changes are coming, ready or not. Death is certain in the journey of the Named One. Death will come often as you walk in your name: death to the ego, to societal expectations, to saying yes when you meant "Hell no." With each death comes a new birthing within you. Each shedding gives way to new perspectives and vision, new wisdom, and a new journey. Death's purpose is to lighten you, to take the backpack of desire, despair, and longing off your shoulders. You do not even know how tired and sore you are until that burden has been removed. Death happens in an instant, as if a Band-Aid is pulled off to reveal healed skin. A small ouch and then relief. The key is in letting death do its work and letting go of old structures, beliefs, and behaviors. Resistance to birth or death will take you off of your path. You can never stay the same as you are in any moment if you truly want more peace.

Sacred Words to Revolutionize Your Life

There are words that are so sacred that when spoken with their original and pure biological nature of truth, beauty, and love they gift you these qualities. They have their own song that will sing you home into your original nature. These are the words that your soul would speak. When I first heard these words in a dream I said, "No, not those." The words were *holiness, reverence, communion, benevolence, glorious, devotion,* and *divine.* I batted them out of my mind and blocked my heart. The words were too religious-sounding for me. What would people think of this Native woman using language derived from the staples of religion? But the truth is pure and insistent. Your dream of what you will do isn't the same dream your soul asks of you.

Resonance means to feel the full and deep reverberating sound. When something has resonance, we are aligned with it even if the choosing mind doesn't care for it. Something deep within us, our soul, resonates with it. In his book *Power vs. Force,* renowned psychiatrist and consciousness researcher David R. Hawkins describes a study in which he gave a Nazi sympathizer two photo images, each in a separate sealed envelope: one of Abraham Lincoln, and one of Adolf Hitler. Though the sympathizer would have actively chosen Hitler if given the opportunity, when tested in a blind study, his body or his soul resonated only with the photo of Lincoln. No matter what we think we value, our soul is the keeper of what we truly align with.

You have probably experienced for yourself when you have chosen something mentally that was in opposition to what your gut was telling you and it didn't work out well. We are often taught to depend on the mind for directives that are the jurisdiction of the soul. We often don't even believe our own experiences until we see that someone else has had a similar experience. Isn't that crazy? Science is beautiful, but it is also a form of numerical philosophy. It's such a pragmatic approach to life. Often in our linear world, we believe that we can only scientifically prove things, when in reality proof is as made up as anything else we believe is real. I am not diminishing the work of science. I am asking you to look within to the places inside where you have experienced a higher level of resonance with the power of energy and vibration, and you either nixed it or kept it secret because it could not be proved. You are the proof. Let that be more than enough.

Words are, like all things, energy. We, both speakers and listeners, determine the energy vibration and send it flying toward one another. Just because we are comfortable with certain words doesn't mean the energy of those words is aligned to us. Think of alignment as belonging. There are words that belong to you. They will speak your soul's truth. They will quiet your ego's lie and they will expand your breadth and depth of experience. Take a moment to intentionally put back into your system some verbal resonance.

Whatever allegiance or aversion you have to these sacred words, let it fall away. Allow the words to scribe back a divinity of yourself that the ego has worked diligently to erase or hide from you. Resonance and dissonance are the soul's meters for what aligns or not. Whatever you believe you understand of these words let it be written anew. With each of these sacred words you can expect to experience expansion in empathy, connection, forgiveness, and allowance—all that forms the definition of what it means to be courageous and vulnerable.

After I released resistance and accepted that I felt the resonance of the words I encountered in my dream, I had to be sure the resonance could be felt by others. I asked 15 people from all corners of the world to help me test their relevance after reading about kinesiology in Dr. Hawkins's *Power vs. Force*. In kinesiology, one uses the body to measure resonance and dissonance. You may have seen this work before where someone puts their arm out in the air at shoulder height and is asked a question. If there is resonance, the arm holds firm as the tester attempts to push it down. Dissonance is when the arm falls toward the hip when pushed. You have a spiritual body of wisdom with you; use it.

Much of your likes and dislikes are based on your historical experiences. Your body, however, has a different reference: your soul. Do you really want your younger interrupted self making decisions for your adult self? These ways of thinking and kinds of choices from yesterday are ways we pretend we are protecting ourselves when we are really locking ourselves out of our own life. Beware. It can be challenging to be told the truth by our souls when our minds have been in control for so long. Our minds have learned the skill of justification. We hold tight to that which we believe comforts us.

Using Dr. Hawkins's blind-envelope method, I sent 10 words in sealed envelopes to a diverse group of volunteers that consisted of Generation Xers, Millennials, Baby Boomers, and others. They represented individuals defined as religious, atheist, or spiritual. There were men and women from several different races and cultures. Among the 10 words were some that you'll see in the practice at the end of this chapter, along with a few negative words such as *hell* and *stupid*.

All the words resonated highly (50 to 72 percent), with the exception of the word *holy*, which resonated among only 30 percent of my test subjects. I concluded that the lack of resonance was because this was the only word that could be used in a defamatory way (holy f***, holy cow, holy s***, etc.). I changed the word to *holiness*. Everyone agreed to retake the test. *Holiness* resonated very high (70 percent). The result indicates that regardless of what someone may have thought of the words had they physically viewed them—for example, an atheist is not likely to self-select a word like *holiness*—the words can still resonate in their body or soul. The study reinforces the old adage, "Don't believe everything you think." None of the negative words resonated above 9 percent. The most important proof, however, is what you prove to yourself. I know the power of words rebuilt my heart when the pain of the world wanted to desecrate me. I know the power of prayer, of laughter, and of touch to restore and reengage my mind with my highest self. Once you have your proof, become the embodiment of it and be dangerous to the mind that wanted to challenge it.

Here are the seven sacred words that will script beauty in you down to the bone. Like a beautiful piece of music, you can attain a lyrical consciousness that journeys you into your soul's knowing. Release, peace, and belonging will come into focus. Don't let the status of grandeur that society has given these words keep you apart from them. They should not be reserved for big moments. Every moment is profound, if only we could see it as such. All moments are equally rich. There are no more special moments for which the china gets taken out. All you ever searched for came with you at birth. Isn't that worth celebrating every day with a vocabulary that represents it? Joy, peace, purpose, and connection are available to you in each moment. Using these words will serve as a connector to your inherent knowing of joy and its companions.

The ego works diligently to make it appear as though these qualities are not present in you, that they are difficult to attain and sustain, are elusive, and should be sought outside of yourself. Diligently attend to your soul's resonance and you will see your altar within.

There is no arrogance in applying these words to you, your life, or others. It is when you are living this vocabulary that you are at your highest service. The ego would have you believe that it is not humble to speak of oneself as holy. The ego is always looking for a way to invalidate you. Each time you agree with the ego, you validate the ego instead of yourself. The ego holds no wisdom, honors no truth, and bears no fertile soil. Humility is needed when you are guided by the ego, because you are not fully aligned with your soul state. When you are fully represented by your soul, peace takes the place of the need for humility.

Each day, consistently pepper your conversations with a few of these sacred words. Over time you will find that you feel more relaxed, at peace, and connected to others. Sometimes just using a sacred word will evoke the world where you desire to belong. Substitute words like *calm* with *peace* and you shall have more peace. Instead of having a good day, might it be a *glorious* day? When isn't a child's laughter *divine*? What difference will you bring to your day with the thought that everyone is *holy*, including yourself? What thoughts would you work to delete if you truly embraced that you are perfectly *holy*? You get to decide right now to be in reverence to all life, especially those people who trigger you. Their forgetfulness, their separation from their holiness, can be restored through you holding them in reverence. Once you start playing with these words, your soul will find other words that have the same high resonance and bring even more love toward you.

It's important to note that though we may not speak harmful words, being judgmental, unforgiving, and resentful are all forms of energetic violence. When we have these thoughts, they are made up of words we energetically put into the world. What we give to others, we give to ourselves. What we think, we believe, and thus, again, we behave. We are consistently showing people what we think of ourselves and of them. What are you showing to yourself? These words will landscape your mind. They will change your mind. Say that sentence again aloud and experience its powerful truth!

When these words found me, five other coaches and I used them in our coaching to observe their impact on clients. Very quickly, we each saw that the clients started using the words. Instead of wanting less stress they were saying, "I'm feeling more peaceful" or "I will bring more peace today to my work." One of my clients began adopting the word *divine* as she spoke about her children. Overall, the handful of clients we worked with found that they were able to be more present. Situations they had once deemed difficult were now easier and less traumatic. Using these words changed the client's perspective, and thus their world. One word can and does change your mind.

Read each word and its definition slowly and then do the practice that follows.

All word definitions, etymology, and year of arrival (which I call *came into* consciousness) are primarily derived from *The Barnhart Concise Dictionary of Etymology: The Origins of American English Words* by Robert K. Barnhart.

HOLINESS

The word *holiness* came into consciousness before the 13th century, having developed from Old English around the year 725. The primary meaning may have been "that must be preserved whole or intact that cannot be transgressed or violated," which would support the relationship to *whole* in Old English.

Definition: That which must be preserved whole or intact.

To recall yourself as whole is to be made holy. What is holy is happy. Holy is internal and external, which means that happiness from it cannot and will not expire like the happiness that you might associate with an event. This is the path you are on. Naming is a restorative and generative journey. You were born whole. You are not broken. Your soul is whole and now with each practice your mind remembers its wholeness. Soon the mind will find itself in agreement with the song of the soul. This may cause an excitement of recognition of your holy state or a deep dread for the same reason, depending on whether your ego or your soul is responding.

We all have our own experience in this lifetime. Certainly, some are fraught with much hardship, while others have an easier time. Each woman and man, whatever their circumstances, is holy. When we forget this, we are more likely to become disengaged with one another and our own life, and can potentially do harm to others. All pain that has ever existed is born from this forgetting, this separation of the holy consciousness. Allowing your holiness to lead doesn't mean you'll end up in a convent. It doesn't want perfection or caution. It wants you to know peace. What will be added in your life when you walk this journey as holy? What creativity will you let fly when you honor your holiness? What will we see in you as you stand in your holiness?

REVERENCE

The word *reverent* came into consciousness around the year 1280, defined as "deep respect"; borrowed from Old French *reverence* ("respect, awe") and Latin *reverentia* ("awe, respect").

Definition: Deep respect for someone or something.

Having reverence for yourself, your life, your medicine, and those of others teaches you presence. It is a deep, abiding connection with holiness. With reverence, you show up with a deep bow. Bowing is a physical acknowledgment of someone or thing worthy of respect.

The downside of technology and social media is the casualness and distance it creates. The casualness of how we articulate ourselves, the messages we leave for others, and the lack of presence and unconscious connection we have when we comment on social media lead to distancing ourselves. Distancing becomes wider when we are absent from the reverence for one another. While the written definition is "deep respect," I think of reverence as evoking deep *loving* respect. Reverence requires us to be energetically connected, meaning we are willing to experience the reverence in another or the reverence needed in the moment for another. It means that we are looking for the reverence. We are waiting for each opportunity to deeply and lovingly respect someone or something. Imagine looking for that opportunity with someone you would normally avoid. If you show up in reverence, you will dismantle the fortress that avoidance built. When we give great reverence, the filters of what we like and don't like fade to the background. Reverence is an honoring of humanity, the planet, and all its inhabitants. It is a teacher of patience, because reverence, like wisdom, is cultivated with time and maturity. What you hold in reverence is what you pay your respect to.

COMMUNION

The word *communion* came into consciousness before the year 1382; borrowed from Old French *comunion* ("community") and Latin *communionem* ("mutual participation"), and derived from the word *common*, meaning "belonging to all."

Definition: Mutual participation; to share thoughts and feelings; to communicate intimately; to be in a state of heightened, intimate receptivity.

We have our humanity in common and we come together to be in communion with it. The commonality is your divinity. You are in relationship to everything and everyone. Your awareness of that will shift the way you interact with life and what you experience. When you engage with life from a place of being in communion, you understand how sacred you and those around you are. The practice of seeing every human as someone worthy to be in communion with is like treating everyone as God. We are all gods in plain clothes. When you consider that you are in communion with the barista, the flight attendant, your partner, and your business colleagues, the ways in which you interact with them will shift. You will see their holiness, and you will bow to it.

I worked with an executive who had a tense relationship with one of his board members. He couldn't find a way to relate to this person. There was no negotiating anything with him; he was stubborn. My client came to me looking for a way to get this board member to move an inch in the direction my client needed him to. I asked him to think of the board meeting as a communion rather than a meeting, and to hold this man and their conversation as holy—to be in holy communion. When you want someone to do something different, you will often find the best results come when you are willing to think differently about the person or the situation. Holding these words in your mind and heart creates an energy like that of a prayer. Prayers are not only requests; at their highest levels they are invocations, appealing to your highest, most loving self to come forward, representing the very thing you asked for.

How does being in communion inform your body, your body language, and what you say or do? How we think of things always informs what we do. Using powerful and sacred language for a powerful and sacred purpose makes change easier and smoother, without the resistance of our negative egos. Yes, we can override these words and the new contextual reality they offer. We can easily white-knuckle through life and hold on to old patterns that suffocate the soul. But why would we?

BENEVOLENCE

The word *benevolence* came into consciousness around the turn of the 15th century; borrowed from Old French *benivolence* and directly from Latin *benevolentia* ("good feeling, good will, with kindness").

Definition: An act to show kindness or good will.

Benevolence is one of those words most people feel don't apply to them and are reserved for saintly people or saintly acts. Words, like people, should never be put on a pedestal. You are well-wishing! You demonstrate acts of kindness and goodwill. Words were created to enable connection to self and others. Never distance yourself from the resonance. Benevolence is a state of grace we bestow on another. You have graced the world with your benevolence. Benevolence is not solely a state of being; it's something you give to another. When you are generous and giving, that is an act of kindness. It is you being benevolent with another. Benevolence is playing games with the child sitting at the table next to yours in the restaurant. It is caring for your parents as they prepare for their last journey on this planet. It is staying present to the teenager who only seems to rant, but you know there is more there. It is giving the homeless woman food and a new coat. It is caring for nature. It is sharing a meal with someone, giving them your time and presence. Benevolence is happening around you and with you all the time. It's happening because of you.

Can you bow into this field of beauty? Noting that you are benevolent is the definition of self-love. It is noting your true spirit. It is not arrogant to honor yourself. Arrogance is falsifying. We each have a holy nature and it is important that you acknowledge yours. We can be quick to give hurts and rejection our full attention and then shy away from self-acknowledgment. Too many times we push away the very self-love we so desire.

GLORIOUS

The word *glorious* came into consciousness around the year 1275 (*glory* arrived even earlier, probably before the 13th century); borrowed from Old French *glorieus* ("glorious, blessed") and from Latin *gloriosus* ("full of glory").

Definition: Deserving of great praise. Marked by great splendor or striking beauty.

To live a glorious life is to approach each day seeing striking beauty in it, even as we also recognize that horrible things happen across the globe every day. Seeing the glorious does not deny a reality—it creates a new one. Can you feel the depth of this word and how it honors you? It commands the head to be upright and the spine to be straight in tall alignment as though it's preparing you to look straight into the glory of it all. Do you see how these words are sacred yet not special at all? They are sacred because they tell you your truth. You are love. You are loved. You are a striking beauty. This day, your smile, your work, is not only good, it is *glorious*. The way a flower blooms, the way snow falls, the way a baby learns to walk, the way you face challenges—these are glorious. Live in your glory and you will bring in gloriousness.

DEVOTION

The word *devotion* came into consciousness around the turn of the 13th century; borrowed from Old French *devocion* ("devotion, piety") and from Latin *devotionem* or stem of *devovere* ("dedicate by a vow").

Definition: Love, loyalty, or enthusiasm for a person, activity, or cause.

Making yourself a vow into the world means you can *fly*. This is not some tightrope, a "Get it right or else you'll be smacked on the knuckles by Father Leary or Sister Mary Margaret." A vow is a high intention of honoring. Devotion is a window looking out onto a meadow that beckons you to come and lie down. Lying in the lush, verdant grass, you are held in communion with your soul. The devout one is open to direct communication to all that ever was. Come to the meadow to consider what you will give your devotion to. Devotion is you waking up each day and donating love to what is important to you. It's an act of supreme loyalty that weds you to that which you cannot stand to be apart from. When you are devoted, you happily edit out those people and actions that keep you from your beloved.

Take a moment to see in your mind the practice of devoting yourself. See it in your mind; now feel it in your body. Experience it fully. Turn up the experience, fill it in with color and sound. What does it mean to live in devotion? What does devotion ask of you? What are you ready to release for devotion?

DIVINE

The word *divine* came into consciousness around the year 1380; borrowed from Old French *divin* ("godlike") and from Latin *divinus* ("of a god"); related to Latin *deus* ("god, deity").

Definition: Godlike.

The word *divine* is a close cousin to *sublime*, an exalted state of being. We encounter these moments often, but just as often we fail to acknowledge them as such. For example, we say, "That book was really good" or "The event was amazing." There are those times when we can pull heaven to earth by naming the situations with the language of the heavens. The intoxicating fragrance of a rose, the majestic beauty of a butterfly, the sweet laugh of a child—all these things are divine. Savoring a delicious piece of chocolate as it melts on your tongue is divine. The divine things in life beg us to slow down and bathe ourselves in them. When we feel the sensual power of ourselves, these are divine moments.

Naming these moments accurately is as important as being named yourself. You become what you call into being. You speak your experience into existence. It has always been so. Everywhere you look you can find the divine. In times of hardship, call on the divine to make itself visible within you and to you.

Even anger has a divine meaning, because it speaks of an unanswered need. Never underestimate your divine, godlike quality. If the word *God* causes you to shirk, let it go; there is no religious affinity here. God is whatever you say it is.

Using resonant wording each day—a little here, a dose there—relieves the repetitive loop in your mind that denies your own divinity. That loop is harmful. Over time, the internal conversation that speaks in terms of limitation, shame, and doubt, toying with your reality—telling you no with such ferocity that it is difficult to deny it—will diminish. Evocative language is a language of yes. Yes, I am wild. Yes, I am dangerous, because I protect my divine nature. Yes, I am beloved. And yes, I belong.

Words are born into the world. They are born into our consciousness as we speak and interact with whatever meaning we associate with them. And, like you and me, they have their own texture; they also have the experience we give them.

Each day you can bring the soul of life forward. In a world that wants to put your soul on pause, you can bring it and its power of illumination forward. As the Named One, your Original Story and Medicine honor the soul of life, even in a world that prefers sanitized, unemotional, spiritless experiences that collapse us into skinny sheets of nothingness. Yes, you can speak life back into any person or situation, even into yourself, with the power of these sacred words. Those who know who they are never compromise themselves with empty language. You are to be heard and seen as you are. Make it a habit to use language that clearly identifies you.

The Practice: Word Resonance

Time: 40 minutes
Materials: journal

In this exercise, bring to mind and heart a worry, a fear, or a terror. Speak one of the seven healing words slowly a few times, allowing for the resonance to be experienced, and listen to the dominion of truth, beauty, and love slowly dissolve the concerns and harms. Speak the word aloud. Your mouth feeling the resonant texture of the word is integral to your physical and emotional experience of it.

The Practice: A Person You Dislike or Fear

Now, do the practice again with a person you dislike. Bring them into your mind. See them in your mind's eye. Bring up the feeling you currently have for them. Anger? Fear? Aversion? Feel that feeling fully. Now breathe three full belly breaths and say a sacred word, such as *communion* or *divinity*. Say it several times, each time allowing the word to do its work. There is nothing for you to do except allow the words to inform your experience of this person. Allow the vibration of the word to wash over and through you, like a gentle rain that wants to cleanse you. Notice if your mind is resisting and giving you reasons why you should hold on to your negative feelings. Remind yourself that you want to be free and that you do not need to hold on to this. Breathe again and say your word as you see this person. Note the shift; it will occur if you are open to it.

Living and Working in the Practice

Replace your everyday words with these sacred words. Practice each day bringing one or two of these words into your vocabulary. Be purposeful, but not careful, and notice the impact on others as they hear the words over time. Notice what you experience when you use these words. Use the words to seed a more loving experience of your world and others.

You will find that over time, long-held beliefs and negative perspectives are released. We don't notice how we put ourselves in prison until we escape from it. We may have believed that someone was unkind to us and sentenced them to life in prison—where they remained, guilty and unable to overturn their sentence. With one word used daily, you free them and yourself. You forgive them and yourself. You bring heaven to your mind.

We are equally unaware of how holding negative thoughts contributes to illness and stress. Using these words doesn't undo what someone has done. But using these words lets us transcend the moment, freeing ourselves and others. You or they are accountable to their own karma. Let that be enough. You do not need to waste your precious resources to hold them prisoner.

I have worked with many leaders and executives to create more communion with their staff. We start with shifting their business language, which can often feel stiff or harsh. For example, no one really wants to be "managed" at work. They want to be supported and engaged. When I'd begin a coaching relationship with an executive, they would invariably ask, "What are my outcomes?" This is an example of a very linear approach to life and work. I would respond with, "What *impact* do you want in your work that you are not having?"

Outcomes has a forced expectation while *impact* is a desire that you bring to life. These words invite a right-brain approach, which is more empathic and connecting.

Below are some everyday words that you can replace with resonant words. Try using these resonant words for a month and notice their impact in you and with others.

Everyday Word	Resonant Word
Nice	Benevolent
Sympathize	Empathize
Stuck	Curious
Calm	Peaceful
Good	Glorious
Special	Sacred
Great	Divine
Appropriate	Congruent
Committed	Devoted
Professional	Integrity
Strategic	Vision
Manage/Management	Engage, Support
Outcome	Impact, Effect

Chapter 9

LIFE AS THE ONE WHO BELONGS

Belonging is an ancient desire that emerged when the earth and our lives were created. It is an essential desire to be emotionally wanted in close proximity and to be held by others in love and in community. Your life literally depends on belonging. Today our physical being isn't as dependent on belonging as it once was, but our psychological and spiritual welfare are intrinsically tied to one another. Belonging isn't commuting from one relationship, event, or group to another. It's also not being locked into someone or something that diminishes you. Belonging lives in the realm of Mitakuye Oyasin—We Are All Related. It's knowing and acting from knowing that all that you experience, all that you are, and all that is, are interconnected. We have a responsibility for all humanity. Your health, your joy, your suffering are dependent on all. It's not as heavy as it sounds. In fact it's lighter to be part of the world in this way. There is a shared responsibility as the Named One that you take on—to care for yourself and others from the healing state of unconditional love. Being in close proximity to unconditional love is vital in belonging because you can be wanted and loved *conditionally* and be ostracized from your tribe. Conditionality isn't your game anymore. Conversely you may pardon people from your life if you cannot belong to them. Those who are afraid of true love and those who still negotiate their love are not your family. You belong to everyone and everything, yet those who do not understand true belonging, those who are afraid of true love, those who still negotiate their love may leave you. Or you may need to leave them. This is part of the path of one who belongs: letting go of people and structures that live in the exterior. Stay next to love; let it hold you tight. Love is your beacon for those on the interior journey to find you. For those who live solely from the exterior, you hold them in love.

Your desire to be emotionally held is paramount in belonging, because it is this internal *knowing* that tethers you to yourself. Being held in love frees you from self-destruction. All suffering begins when we forget our organic indigenous nature. In forgetting, we become separated from our story, medicine, and nature. We begin executing life rather than living in accordance with it. Remembering who you are ends this suffering. You are reunited with your dark and dangerous beautiful nature. You walk with your Original Medicine and live out your Original Story. You do this in relationship to all life and as such you offer your medicinal properties and your story for others to partake. This is the kind of healing you can offer the world simply by the act of truly belonging.

Be Not Alone

We may love our independence, our alone time; we may be introverts and quiet. But knowing that we are loved, that others are waiting for our physical, psychological, and emotional return, allows for us to be free of the anxiety true aloneness brings.

As a Named One, you become adept at discerning and redefining the definitions that society gives you. Societal dictates will often default to the lowest common denominator of intelligence. These are not beautiful messages. A group mentality arises when it engages a low consciousness or unconsciousness. Your sacred nature will see this and you will be called to bring your medicine forward. To stand in your medicine is healing for all. We see examples of the destruction of true aloneness in our world when we walk past the homeless, witness the destruction of people in times of war, or see how a person born with a disfigurement or physical oddity is shunned. We are taught to go against our nature of loving care and to walk quickly past it all. We are taught to abandon our Mitakuye Oyasin nature. And in this, we learn to expect to be abandoned for our own imperfections. This abandonment and isolation decay not only us as individuals but also our society at large. It draws fear and panic close to our own heart as we silently, unconsciously say, while stepping over the man begging for money or food, *There but for the grace of God go I*. This is one way we mismanage our prayer—by not being the prayer for another. Grace has nothing to do with you not being in someone else's shoes; it has everything to do with how you belong to them. The ego is always on the hunt for the interruption, the distance it wants to create from your own godlike consciousness. All fear is a conflict started on behalf of your ego aimed at your soul.

Being named stitches you into belonging. Its decree is this: love all humanity. Being named is not a solo performance to honor only you—it's the marriage of unity. You are wed to all. This is how in belonging you are never alone. You are held by the world and you hold the earth close in your bosom. Do what is yours to do and be there to care for others.

Self-Owning

Naming is the great undoing of the ego. Naming will offer you self-ownership as you choose to step into yourself. This is the self of love. You walk past all that does not inhabit love. Yes, walk right past it. Self-owning says you owe to yourself and the world a vision of what it is to be embedded in a state of love. The ego will have a terrible time of this kind of self-owning. It will say, "You can't ignore the pain of the world; you want to live in a fantasy world where this is no pain?" And your reply will be the silent self-knowing of the vision love gives you. Move forward. What you give value to is what you see and thus create in the world. This is not putting a smiley face on pain. That is the behavior of the ego. This is bringing in love to dissolve the pain.

The experience of belonging comes from our wisest elders who gather us in a circle. In this circle, the elders fill us with their stories of lessons, beginnings, endings, legacies, and medicine. They bring in laughter to heal, stern warnings to keep us safe, pipes to smoke as we say our prayers, and always they bring belonging. Tears of gratitude are dropped back down onto the earth from which they say we come. Songs are sung that tell tales of archetypal and ancient ancestors, to bring them forward to guide us. When we are finished we shake hands, and feast at the table. Perhaps this is why few people know how to walk into belonging, because they don't know any wise elders.

You can be the wise elder for others. Start the circle by sitting in it and light the fire that signals to others to come, sit, and learn. You are being primed to be an elder. Regardless of your age, you are an elder in the making. You will gather us in a circle, telling us your stories and showing us the way to love and peace.

The experience of allowing others to hold you, to see you as you are fully, is the experience of self-owning and belonging. Fall back into the circle as you walk along this journey. Wouldn't you do this for those you love—help them carry their burdens, their joys, their imperfect, perfect soul selves? In fact, you would. Now you discover the beauty of being held. In self-owning, what you learn you teach.

Naming is the great undoing of the ego.

Giving in Belonging

Belonging has as much to do with what you are willing to accept as it does with what you are willing to give. Giving is defined differently in the internal world. In the external world we give away our energy, our finances, and our time to make us feel that we are helping. And sometimes we are. But soon we get tired of giving. Often women are expected to give without ever asking to receive. In the land of belonging, giving is defined as holding your attention and care toward another *and to oneself.* As such, you are receiving what you give. What you give your loving attention to is given within you. You will begin to notice this as you give from this place. This the natural state of evolution.

Giving is the state of presence. So often if we receive, we feel compelled to give something back immediately. Someone picks up the check at dinner, leaves a gift on our doorstep, or introduces us to a potential new client, and instead of fully receiving, fully feeling the love that is being given, we rush to reciprocate. It is difficult to receive without strings, isn't it? Trusting those loving relationships that have already said yes to you is one of the purest acts of generosity. All that is given must also be received by you. What this means is that if you do not receive pleasure and joy in giving, then the giving is done out of obligation. When you learn to really receive from another, you learn what is truly given is not just the thing; it is the love of the giver.

Giving is more energetic than it is physical. It is not simply giving resources or time. You are a conscious, self-trusting, grounded person who can decide when you can give your attention fully and when you can't. Saying no in this context is giving as well because you do not pretend to be present when you can't. When you decide to give, you are extending belonging to the person you are holding. You are holding care for them. For this person, it is like a walk in the bounty of nature filling them up when they need it most.

Giving is as generative to ourselves as it is to others. If what you are doing is not generative, then it is not true giving. Giving is selective—you choose how and when. It's not parceled, but it is conscious. Giving is learned well by giving yourself the same care and attention—the same breath, smile, time, love, gentleness, forgiveness, and reflection that you have given others. As you make this courageous donation to yourself, you will find your capacity to give to others deepens in its intensity and generative powers.

It takes time to know our soul self and to trust our intuition and internal voice. There will be people who betray us, who lie, who steal away our trust and love only to burn it in some wildfire for the sole purpose of seeing a spark they cannot feel within. Occasionally, the ones you trusted with your love and felt that sense of belonging with will let go—sometimes unconsciously, because their own interruptions never got resolved. You, too, have done this to others, which is why you can forgive and move on with your love intact, your suspicions of future relationships deferred, and your internal and intuitive listening deepened, undoubted, and respected. When you truly forgive, you give yourself the peace you so need.

Giving is quality over quantity. It is never about how much you give; it is about *how* you give. As you belong and give of your presence, there comes a time when you pay deep respect to your elder teachers. When the apprentice is ready to be the teacher, you will honor your teachers with a physical gift that says thank you. Should your elders be in spirit form, thank them by being your best you. A verbal gift of gratitude is always received well. In the Native tradition we give a range of gifts: blankets for the person's home or horse, something utilitarian like a beautifully carved knife, water delivery for their home, or chopping wood or even herding sheep! There is a tradition of thanking the elders and announcing your graduation. You are giving to the circle of life in which you belong.

The Writing on the Wall Reads: Authenticity First

Belonging asks for nothing more than your authenticity, which feels very vulnerable. At first it's a raw, timid experience, and then it becomes as simple as walking. It's just what you do. When you do not give yourself over to authenticity, then what you have is the fight of fitting in; your suspicions will be heeded and validated; your heart will require protecting; your intuition will be doubted and the logical mind will take the lead. The expression "fitting in" is a conundrum because you will never fit in. Fitting in should be defined as always trying, always adapting and changing like a chameleon looking to avoid being spotted. The fit one is the one who has pulled a muscle in bravery to access their birthright of belonging. You can decide that you do belong just as you did as a child, never considering for a moment that you do not belong despite evidence to the contrary that your ego will continuously assemble.

The Obstacles of Answering Desire

Desire is delicious to experience and to answer. You've moved from the longing in desire (the ego's path) to belonging from desire. No longer do you live from the insane appetite to have but from a desire for a life filled with passion. Desire is born with you to help you build the fire you will live from. It's an appropriate ache of yearning and longing that you soothe by being who you were born to be in concert with the glorious world. Being who you are born to be is not an individualistic ego approach. It is you taking your threads to intentionally weave beauty into the tapestry of life. In order to answer the desire of you, the desire of belonging, you will overcome some basic but large obstacles that the ego has laid in your path: greed, impatience, unconsciousness, resentment, judgment, comparison, scarcity, and pretense. There are others, but loosening these will set you on your path of self-belonging and loosen the ego's hold. You will come to recognize the ridiculous orders that the ego sends and with ease you will move past the hole in the sidewalk you did not see before. The distractions are many, but your path is defined. It will become easier to distinguish yourself from the noise. You are learning how to train your mind to be in concert with your soul. As you read each of the descriptions, take note of how it appears in your life. This is not an opportunity for shame. You are learning to have great sight.

Greed

Greed isn't often acknowledged at the everyday level. We only look to the larger crimes of greed that are noted in the news. The portal of greed can be easily opened when you believe your desires will not be answered. A greed-based curriculum writes that if you have more—love, money, things, validation, time, children, sex, promotions—you are valid. This noise is so incredibly loud that it hinders your ability to hear the answers of your desires streaming toward you. The noise stimulates a craving for more to fill the hole that you've fallen into. Filling a hole is a job that never ends because its topography is doubt. You don't feel full, so you go for more. Of course, there will never be enough good looks, glamour, shoes, love, money, friends, sex, work, or time. It's an itch that will never be scratched. How do you know what "enough" is?

Impatience

Without the willingness to be seen in our authenticity we become susceptible to other allergens such as impatience. We believe impatience is about not having enough time, but really it's always about being uncomfortable and feeling insignificant. Breathe. What you do not have enough of is yourself—your whole, holy self. Rewrite the story it gives you. Scarcity is not your life or your lot. You are relevant if you choose to believe so. Take notice of what is happening around you. You're missing out by being impatient.

Unconsciousness

Unconsciousness is a privilege in a world in which independence is more precious than interdependence and belonging. It is thinking and acting in "I" instead of "We." It is not noticing your impact. It is an accumulation of irresponsibility. It is not only a world in which you are asleep, but also a world you don't care to wake up to because then others would matter greatly. Those who sleep seek happiness by believing it exists somewhere outside of them. The ego has them trapped and guides them into its store where happiness is sold by events and expires when the event does. In a conscious mind, being joyful is organic. Unconsciousness can take a group of people and make them a dangerous force—think of the Black Friday discount-shopping fiascos when people get stampeded to death. Fear, when not consciously accepted, has the same effect. Remember the Sheffield, England, soccer stadium that became overcrowded with fans at a 1989 match and how people fearing for their lives tried to escape the human crush by stepping on others? Practice being aware of your impact. Are you having the effect you intend in your relationships?

Resentment

Resentment is the antithesis of forgiveness. It is the commitment to being right. When you are resentful you put all your power into a story or scenario that reenacts itself. You are trapped in the past and feeding yourself poison. Resentment fills your taste buds, your sensual experience, with a bitterness you can't wash down. And like anything we hold on to, it eventually becomes us in pathological ways. We become the disease someone gave us. Resentment robs you of one of your most precious human resources: time. It teaches you a false definition of love—that love is for those you like and not for others. Resentment is a statement that you've given up on humanity. Please don't. When you free yourself from this self-imposed jail sentence, imagine what you can do with all the energy you have.

Judgment and Comparison

When we learned about competition at an early age, we simultaneously were taught how to judge others. And as we judged others, we compared ourselves to them. Judgment is a self-inflicted circle of pain. Judgment and comparison dehumanize you, as well as the person being judged or compared. They are triggers for depression, sorrow, and unhappiness. They are acts of violence we do not feel but are nevertheless real. Listen to your mind today and catch your judgments and comparisons. Note the physical experience they are asking your body and mind to hold. When you find yourself casting this kind of hate, breathe and say, "I love you" (if only in your mind). It will make all the difference you need.

Scarcity

Scarcity encompasses all of the above and more. It means forgetting that you are enough. It is the belief that you do not have enough. I'm not talking about true poverty or not having enough food for your children. Scarcity is not a financial statement; it is an emotional one. It is emotional bankruptcy. It lives in a state of fear that paralyzes your creative imagination and keeps you in

THE POWER OF NAMING

lockdown. Scarcity believes in luck and good fortune over soulful desire, willingness, movement, support, and the ability to rise again after failure. Scarcity is poverty of the soul. It steals your organic, abundant nature, engaging you in thinking about what you are not or do not have or can never have or be. Your mind is put on a diet that starves you. There is no faith, no vision, only hysteria. Start by changing your mind. Catch your scarcity thinking and tell yourself a truth you are *willing* to hold on to until you are able to believe it. Look at that truth, feel that truth for others if you cannot for yourself. You can be broke, not knowing where your funds will come from, without feeling poor. You are an abundant, creative soul; act on this.

Pretense

Pretense is making stuff up. Pretending is a lie. It is acting when there is no show and no audience and asking for applause. In the case of belonging, it is pretending you are not ordained by the highest order in this universe to celebrate and live your beautiful nature. Pretending that you are not a glorious human with divine insights, creative brilliance, and a magnitude of depth is not pretty, and it's not the definition of humility. Pretending will not make you safe because you fear visibility. It's like looking at a cupboard full of food and not eating. You are starving yourself. It's being thirsty and not giving yourself the water of life. Pretending to fit in moves you further and further away from the belonging you desire, and with each move away you amputate a piece of you. Please stop pretending. Fitting in costs too much. You may have to leave the culture, the groups, the religion you are in. That is hard and scary, but you are not alone. At first you might feel alone; some journeys are meant to be taken alone, but not for long. To turn away from the known to the unknown is the step taken by each human being who walks in the glory of their nature. Not one person who walks this journey does so without going through a new portal of belonging.

Each of us who steps into belonging becomes a skilled weaver by moving through these portals. The weave of our collective work holds each of us. It holds you as you begin your journey of freedom and naming. You are not free falling. From here your sight is clearer and more brilliant than it has ever been. Your choices are yours, not theirs. Your movement is aligned with your highest thinking. Your movements may be bold or shaky at first, but as you move along your path, you will find that your footing is firm, grounded, and centered.

Turning into Trust

The ego does not want you to trust yourself or to trust that you can be named into your own glory. But you are ready to trust what you know, who you are and what you are not, what is complete, and what will come. Trust is your new ally. Trust that you are wanted. Trust that you belong. Trust that you have the capacity to live the life you see. Trust is faith married to belief. Have faith in your own humanity and believe in it so much that you become it. Trust your intuition. No one ever trumps their own internal voice. Trust your experiences to guide you and trust that you can rewrite most of the negative ones if you want to. Trust your Council of Elders' guidance. Trust that the work you have done here is complete and need not be revisited. Those who trust extend their hands out to the unknown, saying, "Take me with you." In trusting the unknown you delete the scenario-making mind that wants to anticipate every outcome and prepare for battle.

You no longer need the mental gaming of scenarios. You don't have to fight with life. You are the bringer of light and of life. You've put down your swords to hold the cup of life in love. Isn't that just wonderful? Life will never be perfect. Perfection is not the aim or desire of the Named One. Love is yours to claim in a life of belonging, hand in hand, with one another, through it all.

The Practice: Metta Kindness Meditation à la Christi Baker

Time: 10 minutes
Materials: a willing heart

This meditation is about compassion, first for self and then for others.

Get comfortable and take a deep breath.
Now take another.
Picture yourself in your mind's eye.
There you are, perfect.
Take another deep breath.
Then say to yourself:
"May I be happy
May I be well
May I be at peace
May I be free from suffering."

Pause and take that in.
Take three deep breaths.

Now picture someone you are close to—a lover, a spouse, a friend, a family member, a pet.
Hold them in your mind.

Take a deep breath and then wish them well and say to them:
"May you be happy
May you be well
May you be at peace
May you be free from suffering."

Pause and take three deep breaths.

Next, picture someone toward whom you have neutral feelings. That person might be a barista, a neighborhood resident, your mail carrier. Even though you are not closely connected to this person, you know that their well-being is tied to yours.

Be with them in your mind's eye for a moment and wish them well.

Now say to them:
"May you be happy
May you be well
May you be at peace
May you be free from suffering."

Pause as you send that out to them. Take three deep breaths.

Now picture someone with whom you are having a hard time. Be with them in your mind's eye and say to them:
"May you be happy
May you be well
May you be at peace
May you be free from suffering."

Pause and send that out to them. Take three deep breaths.

And last, I want you to take all that loving-kindness you've cultivated so far today and send that out to all beings.

Take a deep breath, and with love, wish them well.

"May you be happy

May you be well

May you be at peace

May you be free from suffering."

Pause and take three deep breaths.

Close this meditative prayer in a way that is comfortable for you.

The Practice: Your Prayer

Time: 30 minutes

Materials: journal and pen

Give yourself a minimum of 30 minutes, knowing that this practice may accompany you for months. Open your journal and begin writing your own prayer. This is a prayer to guide you when you forget who you are (because you will). This is the prayer to bring you back to yourself and to your holy nature.

Amen. Ahe. And so it is.

Chapter 10

DECLARING YOURSELF: WRITING YOUR MANIFESTO AND VOW

Your manifesto is a declaration of what you believe and thus what you are committed to live. It is different from the prayer you wrote in your practice at the end of the previous chapter. The manifesto marks the verbs of your life. It's what the world can count on as you walk in your story and your medicine.

In this chapter, you will also create your vow, which is a single sentence that captures the promise of your manifesto. In writing your manifesto and your vow, you declare yourself to the world. In writing these declarations, you admit that you know your soul's truth and you will not be kept from it any longer. Your manifesto is simple in form, but profound in your experience. It starts simply, with *I believe* . . . or *I am* . . . or both.

A vow is a promise, but it a special kind of promise. It is a solemn pact.

A vow to the soul is made to draw you in closer to yourself. A vow should be something you enter into eagerly. Nothing so heavy that it causes you pain, but nothing so light that no inner muscle is fortified. We make our vows to know ourselves more intimately.

Your vow is a promise to experience your highest, most luminous self in the here and now. Your vow is to know your fullest capacity in the outer world. Your vow is a poem from your soul that your mind has finally acknowledged. In fact, your entire life is a series of poetic lines writing a life of courage, danger, curiosity, hope, joy, grief, and love.

There is potency in our language, and we so often misuse it. In a previous chapter we looked at the generative power of language. That same specificity is called for when you write your manifesto. The words you speak about yourself and to yourself are important for you to recognize your soul's identity. In writing your manifesto and vow, you're calling for your name. What words would you use to call someone you love home? Here words invoke a truth-telling legacy that writes itself into the hem of your soul. When we repeat quotes or mantras we are invoking their deeper extended meanings, yet so many times we use quotes and mantras without even knowing from where they are derived and the depths we are calling forth as we speak them.

The Hidden Truth Is Revealed

Thanks to the work you have done in the previous chapters, you intuitively sense your inner manifesto and vow, though it can be a scary thing to craft. Fear makes great play at hide-and-seek with your inner knowing. Rather than seek your inner knowing, allow it to be revealed. Your true mind, the sane mind grounded in love and what is beautiful about you, holds your truth. There are no more stories that have been written for you by others. Free will is yours and as such you will choose what you will believe and what you will live. What truths are you going to reveal in your vow? Your conscious mind finds creative ways to reflect your truth back to you, from the people and things you cherish and those you envy, in the experiences you fear and those that expand you. Take note of your feelings, because every emotion has a belief substantiating it. What are you drawn to? What do you fear? What aspects of yourself do you share and what do you hide? To complete your manifesto, dip into the corners of your heart and pull out those shadowy pieces you've hidden. Whatever you give air to you give breath and life to.

And Now, a Warning

The story you write is the story that becomes you in the world, this time on purpose. And with purpose comes certain joy and certain destruction. Writing a manifesto declares first to yourself, and next to others, that you will not be negotiated with. It promises that old structures and behaviors will cease to exist. Evolution is thorough. As you evolve into your name, new partners, behaviors, thoughts, and speech will emerge. Evolution generates congruence. You are inviting death. The death you are evoking is only for the weeds you no longer want. There will be relationships that come to an end. You will grieve. You may be angry for a moment. There are things you do now that won't work for the you who is emerging, and this can be very frustrating. You will feel like banging your head against a wall. Thoughts you held for so long will transform. This will delight and surprise you, but it might not have the same response from others who shared your former beliefs and opinions.

I know, I know, we want change as long as nothing has to be disrupted. We want our naming to be a seven steps kind of process to be completed in a weekend course. But just as your name will teach you how to honor yourself and to do so without compromise, the soul isn't negotiating its process either. Anything that truly expands and deepens you needs space and time to do so.

So what do you do? Hold on while the earthquake called your life happens? Yes, hold on. But not too tightly. You'll need freedom to look around at the destruction, to take it in, to turn over the gems you once cherished, toss them into the rubble, and accept that this is the end of a disconnected self. You'll need your intuitive self and soul self to continue walking the path of "you" and to remain invested in curiosity for the sake of what is coming. A friend who supports your growth will be a lifesaver. It's imperative to remember this is what you asked for. You asked for a recontextualizing of your life by way of a name. In accepting that you called this forth, you also acknowledge your power. This is the path of surrender. You can walk this path.

The Beauty Way prayer from the Navajo people declares beauty is present to our senses, though our mind may only see destruction. It is a directive to be the experience of beauty. Like the Beauty Way, your manifesto and vow are a type of prayer you will walk into the world. There is nothing to be feared. Hold close to your vow and manifesto, hold close to those who support this new you whirling into creation.

The prayer for death is the prayer for new life. This is the prayer you will walk.

The Beauty Way Prayer

In beauty may I walk.
All day long may I walk.
Through the returning seasons may I walk.

Beautifully will I possess again.
Beautifully birds . . .
Beautifully joyful birds.

On the trail marked with pollen may I walk.
With grasshoppers about my feet may I walk.
With dew about my feet may I walk.

With beauty may I walk.
With beauty before me, may I walk.
With beauty behind me, may I walk.
With beauty above me, may I walk.
With beauty below me, may I walk.
With beauty all around me, may I walk.

In old age wandering on a trail of beauty, lively, may I walk.
In old age wandering on a trail of beauty,
living again, may I walk.

It is finished in beauty.
It is finished in beauty.

Can you feel the texture of this poem-prayer? How it wants to write itself into you? In each line there is acceptance, affirmation of what is so—that beauty dwells in and around you. When you declare yourself, it is done, there is no argument, no proof required. Living your manifesto is the period at the end of the sentence and you will walk in beauty.

Joaquin's Manifesto Story

Joaquin came to me looking for an uncompromising connection to his body of work as an executive coach. There are thousands of coaches in the world. It's a crowded and misunderstood field. So many people call themselves coaches. What does that even mean? With so much competition, he wasn't clear on how to definitively and uniquely represent himself. It was imperative that he be able to speak the difference he would bring. Uncompromising. Definitive. Clear and representative of his unique qualities. On the path to naming, Joaquin wrote his manifesto to call forth his soul's knowing. The manifesto was his way of spilling the truth of his convictions and remembering what he wanted to honor is his life and his work. Here now, is Joaquin's (he is named Hermès, the Messenger) manifesto.

- I am a source being—greater than my mind and its ideas.

- I am a powerful life leader who creates and lives life deliberately.

- I follow my heart and soul's desires.

- I share my gifts and talents with the world without apology or shyness.

- I am here to show my kids that it is possible.

- I am a successful and inspirational leadership coach, speaker, and author.

- I am connected to my soul and trust my intuition.

- I live in integrity with my feelings, intentions, and actions.

- I surrender to life and let go of the fear.

- I stand tall in life.

- I am the hero of my life and my best friend.

Joaquin's manifesto is a simple and clear reminder of who he is and what he will be in the world.

The Practice: Writing Your Manifesto

Time: 30 minutes
Materials: journal and pen

I have never named anyone before they have been willing to declare themselves. It's an impossible request. How can someone know their name until they speak what they stand for?

On the Red Road there are a series of smaller ceremonies one must participate in, sometimes for an entire year, before being invited to the more spiritually demanding ones. The continued participation of the less-demanding ceremonies reunites one with their soul and the capacity for more truth. You have been working up to this. Your manifesto generates a written and verbal agreement with your soul to "be on purpose." Being on purpose, this alignment with soul self, lays the groundwork for the initiation of your naming. Transformation begins one sentence at a time. Once you announce your

175

truth it is difficult, painful even, to betray it. This is the audacity of love.

Write simple sentences in the form of declarative statements.

I believe . . .

I am . . .

I cherish . . .

I commit . . .

As you write your manifesto, notice what is being birthed into consciousness. Take your time. Walk in this with a slow, deliberate pace, but don't mentally churn your wheels either. Notice who is writing your manifesto. Let your soul take the lead; leave your mind to rest. Give yourself 10 declarations and call it a day. And for goodness' sake, don't wordsmith it to death.

Let it sit for a bit, then pick it up and speak it aloud. Does it resonate? Does it scare you just a little? (This is the litmus test for resonance.) Is it you speaking, or what you think you should say? Is there more? Now put it down. Walk away from it and see if it calls you to pick it up and live it. Do two or three rounds of picking up and putting down. It will take a few rounds for your lips to agree to this conviction, for your mind to surrender to it, and for you to feel the cartwheels of joy your soul is doing.

Baring It All in Diapers

In every naming session there comes a time when I tell my clients, "This is your Depends adult underwear moment. We're about to go into dark territory. Your manifesto must be shared to be fully declared." I know, we like making vision boards that no one will see and writing poetry that no one will hear. We like *pretending* we are present and accounted for. We love hiding or being over-the-top verbose and this is none of that. Sharing yourself is what love does. Love shares itself, trusting it will be held by the love of others. It's a brave thing to be loved. You can do this. You can.

Put on your big girl/boy panties and go tell your tribe. Make a video, post it to folks who can hold this expansive place you are stepping into. Go ahead, let them cheer you on. We need witnesses to bare ourselves to. It is both brave and humbling. The vulnerability to share your manifesto, and later your vow—out loud—makes it real. It's not that these folks will hold you accountable, it's that having had the courage to say it *you will hold yourself accountable.* Step into yourself. Beauty can't be cloaked. The spoken and written word together are a power the personality of you cannot wrestle down. There is only a certain amount of space on the stage called you. The more you take up, the less room there is for that which is not you.

In case you read through those last few paragraphs with flurry of panic, I'll say it once more: You simply must share your manifesto with those who can hold your story. Share it with those who will love you. Some people have chosen to post their manifestos to YouTube. Some have done so quietly, others brazenly, as if to dare the world with, "Oh yes I am, yes I do, yes I will." Whatever style you choose, there is deep humility in bowing one's head down to mark one's appearance on the stage of life. And one never leaves until the crowd completes its applause. It would be rude to do otherwise. Breathe.

The Vow

Like a mantra, your vow is both simple and profound. It makes a succinct statement and sits atop a deeper conversation.

Joaquin's Vow

I promise to act in integrity, to hold the best of intentions, to move forward and grow.

My vow: I vow to belong to one another and to walk in beauty.

Beware, there will be other shiny objects calling for your attention. Other creative endeavors so brilliant you will be lured away to listen to them instead of your vow. You may tell yourself this is silly, call it child's play, that it has no value. You will be called to be brilliantly intellectual about it. You will be matter-of-fact about it. These are tools of the ego, to pull you away from your purpose and back into the world of uncertainty and compromise.

Your small self, the ego, wants you to believe that there isn't much for you to do or understand, just try a little and you'll get a lot. But the soul has a richer request. The soul only asks for you to be willing to know yourself anew. Actually, the power of naming wants you to unlearn everything you *think* is relevant to reveal exactly what *is* relevant. But who will you employ, your soul or your ego? Which wolf will you feed?

The Practice: Writing Your Vow

Time: 10 minutes
Materials: journal and pen

Your vow is a single-sentence statement of who you will be in the world. It is meant to be the North Star you turn to should you get lost. It is the master prayer. When people pray for peace they believe the only wars are the wars "out there." Uncertainty, compromise, fear, pretense—these tumultuous states are our inner conflict. Your vow is the call of peace.

Speak your vow aloud. What is its bottom-line promise? Perhaps you know this vow, this truth. Sit with paper in hand and record what you have always known.

Use no more than 15 words. More words won't bring about more clarity. You know your vow; you're already living it to some degree. Think of it like the symbol of the wedding ring that promises commitment. The vow is what you promise to yourself and to this beautiful world.

So, off you go. Settle in for it all: the fear, excitement, earthquakes, acceptance, and birth. Just start writing. You know this. You do.

Chapter 11

BE NAMED

Who are you, wise one? What will you admit to yourself and to the world? The power of naming belongs to the power of owning. No one who gets named in the traditional ceremony walks away shy, distant, embarrassed, or feeling it's too big for them. Being named is being seen. You are ready to be seen. Every child, every man, and every woman needs to be seen, needs to be received. Being named is an act of love.

You have stripped away what kept you in the past. You now are walking with your Original Story and Medicine. You have honored and bowed to you dark, dangerous, and beautiful nature. As you continue to live into your spiritual practice, being and walking as the Named One is a humbling experience. Humility is a part of your medicine bundle. Being humble is the simple act of remembering to bow your head to all life. We are all equal. Bowing is not an act of self-diminishment. Beyond honoring your name you have also agreed to honor the spirit of all life. Being named means that you join in a sacred and holy communion with all that is and all that has ever been. You are the world's sanctuary. You are its grace, its fire starter, its lover, and its protector. Your prayers and your life are one.

Naming in Community

Naming is meant to be done in communion. In a traditional naming ceremony, you are named by the one or ones who see you. It is this gift of being seen, of being received, that calls forth the poem written within you. The tribe that names you is the one that holds you in love. They are the ones who will teach you how to challenge your fear, bow to your soul, and honor what is sacred, dark, dangerous, and beautiful. Courage is not a solitary act. We are encouraged to become our greatest vision of ourselves as we watch others around us stand tall, and even when we see others who refuse to get up and get on with life. Courage is encouraged by those around us.

The rules of etiquette at every ceremony ask that you bow in respect for those who support you, for the sacred ceremony, and for your own soul. When you ask your tribe mates to see your vision, witness your story and medicine, and then name you, do so with humility.

There are three naming ceremonies for you to consider: the Gathering of the Tribe Ceremony, the Council of Elders Visualization Ceremony, and the Dream Catcher Ceremony. Each ceremony is one in which your name comes from others. None of these are linear or mental exercises. Ceremonies are intended to serve the one who is being honored, to confer healing, and for those in attendance to witness the evolution of the one being named and to be healed by extension. Wherever a naming ceremony takes place, it is done in the Creator's presence and with the Creator's blessing. There is preparation and etiquette for the Named One and for those who will be conferring the name. Together you and your tribe, in communion and in reverence, are bringing heaven to earth.

Guidance on Ceremonial Etiquette

In the traditional way, I've been taught to offer my elders tobacco. The tobacco offering means I have something I need to ask of them. If the elders accept my offering I then sit with them and ask for what I need. I put no parameters on how what I need will be delivered. (For a list of common offerings and gifts for elders, refer back to Chapter 9.)

Your naming is so important that you need to create space both before and after the ceremony. You may want to fast and spend a day in quiet contemplation or prayer. Take a look at the world as you prepare and consider how you will care for it and its inhabitants now. As you prepare do your best to not sandwich the naming in between other events. You have to give yourself the space to walk between worlds now. This is not a time to post on social media. This is a humbling, private ceremony. Some things are meant to be kept close in. Give yourself, your community, and the ceremony the respect it deserves. The ceremony is still occurring within you long after it's officially over. Be gracious with yourself. Allow the ceremony and the name to inform you. At the same time, don't make it a central focus. Integrate your new self and carry on with life.

At the completion of a ceremony, an offering of gratitude is made to those who have held you and named you. Gift them with love. Care for them and they will continue to care for you. Gifts of gratitude should be personal to the recipient. In the traditional way, we offer our gifts, such as blankets, items needed in the home, or money, and a handshake and it is done—kind of. Unlike the Western world where we over-thank people so as to erase an imagined debt, in the tribal world once someone has given you a ceremony, they are your family. Keep them in your heart and prayers and take care of them when they are in need.

For Those Who Will Be Conferring the Name

The ceremony can begin casually with each person telling a story about the one who will be named. For example, they can share how they came to know you and what their own impact is in the world. As the sacred space settles, those in the circle can share their wisdom teachings for the one who will be named. They can share their expectations and describe how they will count on the Named One. What characteristics do the elders see for you to embrace? What are they proud of? If you are participating in someone else's naming ceremony you have the responsibility similar to that of a godparent.

Gathering of the Tribe Ceremony

Call on those who are ready to walk this path with you; those who have read this book and have done the work are your clan. Gather together to create your naming circle. No more than two people should be named in a single ceremony. Ceremony takes as much psychological energy as it does physical and spiritual energy. Everyone should be fully present to each naming. Holding too many ceremonies is spiritually exhausting. You may decide to do this in stages. Create a sacred space. Traditionally a fire is lit. A fire calls the circle into being and signals that the ceremony has begun. You can build an altar to hold your candles, a symbol for the fire. In the Native tradition it is common for us to laugh and tell jokes before the profundity of the ceremony starts. This is important as it takes the edge off and humanizes us. Once we begin, we shift into the sacred space a naming ceremony demands. You can start your ceremony by making an offering to your people. Give them enough context to see who you are. You may want to share with them:

- What is important to you about being named
- Your Original Story and Original Medicine
- Your dark, jeweled nature
- Your prayer
- Your manifesto and vow

In the Native way it is not uncommon for our elders to ask us what name we desire, but be warned that does not mean you will be named as such. Often it is just a prompt. Many elders would never defer to you for a name. At the conclusion of the ceremony and before the feast, offer your gifts to each person. Typically there is a feast after the ceremony, but you may celebrate in community any way you like. Though you are encouraged to do this in person, if you need to do it virtually make every effort to see others' faces via a video conference.

Council of Elders Visualization Ceremony

If you choose to do this ceremony yourself, make sure you are doing it because you feel that it is yours to do. Make sure you are not avoiding being vulnerable. You may want to revisit the work you did on your Council of Elders in Chapter 7.

This type of ceremony is yours to do if your name has either already come, or if you can feel it is close. Because this a visualization process, it is yours to do alone. You can also decide to enfold the Council of Elders into a community naming. Should you go it alone, you may want to share the name with your people later in an introduction and a celebration.

Meet with your council before the ceremony to ask them to name you. Ask them how you should prepare for the ceremony and what they need to go forward. You may not need to tell them your story, manifesto, and vow because your elders are with you all the time and know your journey well. Your elders will prepare you for your ceremony. Circle up around the fire. Make your tobacco offering to the fire in your visualization. Be present, be grateful, listen fully, and be named. At the conclusion, shake your elders' hands. Walk in beauty.

Dream Catcher Ceremony

If you are the kind of person who often gets directives from the dream world, then this ceremony will honor the spirits who speak to your conscious mind during dreamtime.

Similar to a vision quest, this ceremony often takes four days to complete. Each night take at least 20 minutes to speak to your conscious and subconscious mind. Speak about your visions for yourself and how you are ready to be the Named One. Imprint your mind with images, words, songs, or other sounds from your soul. Put something beautiful in your mind such as a poem or a mantra. Keep a journal close by to capture what you hear and see. You don't have to wake fully to scribble down what you heard or saw. I promise you, you will be astounded by what your subconscious mind will reveal to you when your brain is quiet. Should you wake between the hours of 2 and 5 A.M., don't go back to sleep. Stay up and listen. Chief Joe Chasing His Horse would say, "When the spirits come, give them your attention." Speak and listen to them. This is real. The days of second-guessing the downloaded information you receive are over. Your creative mind, your vocabulary, and your perspectives will widen and deepen when you listen well.

When you hear your name, accept it with gratitude and offer a gift to the earth-based world as a way of thanking the elders. Your ego may want to negotiate your name by telling you it's not right or it's too much or you made it up. Stay centered. Stay committed to your soul's truth. Stay quiet and breathe. Breathing means you are alive and as such you are agreeing to be present and accounted for. The ego wants you to hold your breath, clench your teeth, and tighten your belly, all of which are psychic and metaphysical representations of death. The death on behalf of the ego hopes for a mental war where you talk back to it, explaining yourself, justifying your name—but you are done with battles and war. You have heard your name and you now walk on the path of love. You belong to those who are named and they belong to you. You live in a state of consciousness that moves you through the squandering of your energy that the ego wants for itself. You never again have to speak into any conversation that is not honoring of humanity. Later, consider creating a gathering of those people who hold you to introduce yourself and share your name. Walk in beauty.

It Is Done

Whichever ceremony you have held, you are now the Named One. Say your name aloud. Let your eardrum drill it into your body. Let your body recognize your name. Give your body and your mind time to catch up to what your soul already knew. Now your soul and mind follow the sun together. You and the light of the world are one. There are no walls between you and love. Walk with love.

Now you know the preciousness of each day and of your life. You know its depth and breadth, but you also know its brevity. You are the vessel for all wisdom. You now see why the elders are proud to walk with wisdom etched on their faces. There are those who grow old and there are those who become wise. Wisdom has its own landscape of beauty and it wants to walk with and in you. Walk in beauty as the wise ones before you have. It is done. Rest and rest well. Take time to let yourself mingle quietly in the forest of your soul. There you will find many paths to journey upon, each with its own story to tell you. Journey well. For the naming is done and it was done well.

Your Ceremony

Bless this reunification with the sacred heart.

Know yourself as holy and loved.

May you see yourself as wanted in the circle of all life.

Awaken each morning and to each moment as the One Who Is Loved.

May you know you are safe to be you.

May you give safe passage to others.

Know you belong at the fire.

Tend to your internal flame well.

May you walk the path of becoming an elder.

Bless your scars, your failures, and your hardships the way you bless your fortunes.

May you live a life of many chapters.

Speak kindly, write powerfully, sing loudly.

Follow your heart, not the impression of others.

Give yourself every chance in every moment and never despair.

Know that help is at your beck and call.

May you know your own voice and share it well.

May you live and walk in the joy of life.

May humility be your companion.

Bow to all the inhabitants of Mother Earth, for they belong to you and you to they.

Stand in your authority.

May you start the fire for others.

The Practice: Bestowing Your Name

The above ceremonies are just ideas. You know what your soul desires. Allow your spirit to imagine exactly what you need and want. You may decide to go out in nature to listen for her input. Perhaps a day of quiet solitude is in order. Or you can turn to your group or a friend who can help you design your ceremony. Whichever path you take, do so with clarity that this is *your ceremony*. This is about you and for you. This is a sacred ceremony and you are its center. Embody this name. Believe this name. Be this name. You are a prayer in this world. It has always been and now you know it.

What impact do you want this name to bring forward?

What will you behave into the world?

What danger will you bring and for the sake of what?

What else will you let go of for you who are named to live brightly?

Who are your earthly guardians and how will they support you as you move forward?

Ahe, We are all related.

Chapter 12

LIVING AS THE NAMED ONE: WALKING BETWEEN TWO WORLDS

It is done. You remember who you are. That is all that the universe, the Creator, ever wanted for you—to be reunited with the remembering of your soul love and soul knowing. From this knowing you gift the world with your medicine. The journey of the Named One is holy. It is one of intention and purpose. It is the path of emotional and spiritual maturity. It is the path that every elder has walked. The naming ceremony only confirms what you already knew but may have forgotten or been asked to forget. Never again will you be turned away from your internal compass. You need never look outward for directives. As the Named One, you have fresh priorities, such as tending to yourself and to your spirit. Listen for the applications of your Original Medicine. Notice when your Original Story is ready to write new chapters. Know who is wise enough or to hold these with you and who isn't. This road is narrow in focus and determination yet broad in application and possibilities. The road will take you to all the places you need to go. May you travel well.

You have been blessed and you are the blessing. Everything you see going forward will in some way be blessed and named by you. This is the way of the Named One. Take your life seriously—don't waste energy on the things that don't nourish your soul. Leave behind what tries to cling but has no purpose. Don't take life too seriously; don't make it so profound that you abandon belly laughter, slow walks, or dark chocolate. We Named Ones are a playful bunch. When you walk between the two worlds, the earth and the spirit, you learn that play and laughter are as important as intention.

Gather with your tribe often. You will need them on this walk of life to steady you and to remind you, should you wander off. They will speak your language, support your intent, reframe what you might call failure, and make you laugh when you get caught in self-importance.

This is your path now. You will journey between the earth and spirit realms as you meet with your Council of Elders, as you live your life, and as you do your work. Your work—be it a janitor, editor, teacher, or executive—will be profoundly influenced by your Original Story and Medicine. Everything you do now is a prayer you put into the world. Those are the words my chief said years ago, that I say to you right now. You are the prayer by doing nothing more than being you. Make no mistake, this is not the path of burdens; this is the path of freedom. You are free to be exactly who you are. Anyone who is freed to be themselves heals the pain and suffering of the world. This is how your Original Medicine works. This is why you don't have to go save the world or heal others. Your freedom is healing for you and others. Walking between two worlds will take practice and support. Walking in the realm of the spirit is comforting, even enlightening, and it will be tempting to stay there, but you have a purpose here on earth. The practice is to bring heaven on earth, to pull the spirit with you. When you come back to the physical world, it can be disorienting and confronting. I used to call my uncle Pablo and say, "The landings are hard." Pablo was one of my lifelines, someone to help me ease back into a hard world. Michele Justice, my Sundance sister, would continue to remind me to bring the prayers back with me and weave them into my life and work. You will need those people who can steady you. Those people who remind you who you are because though you are named, life can and will continue to throw curves at you. There are few things to cling to as you move forward. We should all cling to what is precious in life.

Cling to Your Spirit

Clinging to your spirit does not mean you have to guard or protect it as you might have done before. Be consciously aware, having clear boundaries and being consistent in your thoughts, words, and deeds. Boundaries are for you and others. Clear boundaries are created from knowing what you value and living in concordance with your values. Self-nurturing becomes a daily practice. Nurture yourself by slowing down your pace. Redefine the glorification of "busy." Opt for a full life rather than a busy one. Taking deep breaths often cures more than you may realize. Worry is an act of treason against yourself. Time isn't real, so don't manage it or let it make you crazy. If you are a parent, who you are and what you do is always being modeled for your child. Practice nurturing with them. Daily meditation and meeting your Council of Elders will refresh your thoughts and center your mind into your heart. Nurturing yourself is part of your Original Medicine.

Cling to Love

Because you are free to be, you are free to love deeply. We are trained out of loving freely and taught conditionality. The lessons of loving freely and deeply are often hard won. We love and our hearts get broken. Patched up but not healed, we put our toes in the water of love and cross our fingers. As you walk this path you are safe to release all hurts, turning them in for a redeemable perspective named faith. Have faith in the healing properties of love. Love is not a currency that is traded. Love is never conditional. You know what conditionality feels like. Love teaches you that you can love others closely or from a distance. Love never puts you in harm's way, nor is it careful. Love is conscious. Love finds the love in another and sends love down that path. Love sees who the other is and lets them be that. Love sees their interruptions and pauses and accepts them. Love doesn't *try* to heal; it *is* the master healer. Love teaches you how far to go in with another. Love is omnipresent. Love never needs protection because love is protection.

A Blessing: May You Travel Well

May you walk in love of life and self.
May you have conversations with laughter.
May you know your worth and never sell it.

May you sing the poem scribed into your soul.

May you love the life you grow.

May you always be who you are.

May you speak with kindness to yourself.

May you give your art life.

May you say no as deliberately as you say yes.

May you see your beauty.

May you be an excited pupil of your wild and dark nature.

May your heart be free to love all.

May your dreams remind you of your divinity with wild and beautiful portraits and ecstatic landscapes.

May you take notice of your soul's bow to you as you walk your way.

May you travel well.

In Beauty, It Is Done

It is done. You are named. You have accepted responsibility for all life—an easy undertaking as the Named One. Stay within close range of nature and you will never forget your own. Give of your love without any stickiness and your love will be returned in surprising ways. I've heard many warriors say, "Today is a good day to die." My interpretation is: When you have lived a good life, a life of love and grace, when you gave and were able to receive, when you've walked in alignment with your highest nature, you can die fulfilled. Don't wait to be happy when X, Y, or Z happens. Be happy now, because you want to. Don't wait to be successful; own that you are right now. Don't wait to be loved. Be loved by all of us.

The Practice: Closing

Time: Be generous and give yourself a minimum of 30 minutes
Materials: none

Now you know that a practice is something you do each day. Practice your meditation and prayers each day. Bless yourself in this way and you bless the world. Ask your guardian angels for support and open your eyes to see the beautiful world that passes most people by. You walk in two worlds now. Do not give hate and disorder your attention.

This can be hard to understand at first. It does not mean you do not know what is occurring in the world. It means you do not feed and absorb something that is not love. Make your mind a sane one. Do not fight with the drunkard who is not in his right mind. Stand in your authority to love. Dr. Martin Luther King, Jr. was one of many who beautifully modeled bringing heaven to earth. At the forefront of one of the ugliest wars—racism—he did not confront it; he altered it. Everything you need is in your mind. Tend to that landscape daily. Do not wait for droughts or floods to come. Stay present to your mind. Read your manifesto and vow often. This is your lifelong practice. We all get better at anything we practice in life, love, and spirit.

It's a great day to die—and to live.
Walk in beauty.

Mitakuye Oyasin

ABOUT THE AUTHOR

In her writing, coaching, and speaking, Melanie DewBerry brings the wisdom and teachings of her Native American elders to others. Melanie's African American and Native American heritage instills in her a stance of perseverance and the desire to live life purposefully. She holds a master's degree in Asian Economic Development and Political Risk, and is a veteran coach of 18-plus years; for 10 of those she was the senior lead trainer for the largest coaching school in the world, the Coaches Training Institute. Melanie is also an international speaker and has given TEDx talks in Austria and Canada. She uses the power of spirituality, language, words, and naming to remind us all how we belong to one another. Website: www.melaniedewberry.com

For more bonus materials, including visualizations, blessings, and more, visit www.melaniedewberry.com/PONvisuals.

Username: soul
Password: naming

We hope you enjoyed this Hay House book. If you'd like to receive our online catalog featuring additional information on Hay House books and products, or if you'd like to find out more about the Hay Foundation, please contact:

Hay House, Inc., P.O. Box 5100, Carlsbad, CA 92018-5100
(760) 431-7695 or (800) 654-5126
(760) 431-6948 (fax) or (800) 650-5115 (fax)
www.hayhouse.com® • www.hayfoundation.org

Published and distributed in Australia by:
Hay House Australia Pty. Ltd., 18/36 Ralph St., Alexandria NSW 2015
Phone: 612-9669-4299 • *Fax:* 612-9669-4144 • www.hayhouse.com.au

Published and distributed in the United Kingdom by:
Hay House UK, Ltd., Astley House, 33 Notting Hill Gate, London W11 3JQ
Phone: 44-20-3675-2450 • *Fax:* 44-20-3675-2451 • www.hayhouse.co.uk

Published and distributed in the Republic of South Africa by:
Hay House SA (Pty), Ltd., • P.O. Box 990, Witkoppen 2068
info@hayhouse.co.za • www.hayhouse.co.za

Published in India by: Hay House Publishers India,
Muskaan Complex, Plot No. 3, B-2, Vasant Kunj, New Delhi 110 070
Phone: 91-11-4176-1620 • *Fax:* 91-11-4176-1630 • www.hayhouse.co.in

Distributed in Canada by: Raincoast Books,
2440 Viking Way, Richmond, B.C. V6V 1N2
Phone: 1-800-663-5714 • *Fax:* 1-800-565-3770 • www.raincoast.com

Take Your Soul on a Vacation

Visit www.HealYourLife.com® to regroup,
recharge, and reconnect with your own magnificence.
Featuring blogs, mind-body-spirit news, and
life-changing wisdom from Louise Hay and friends.

Visit www.HealYourLife.com today!